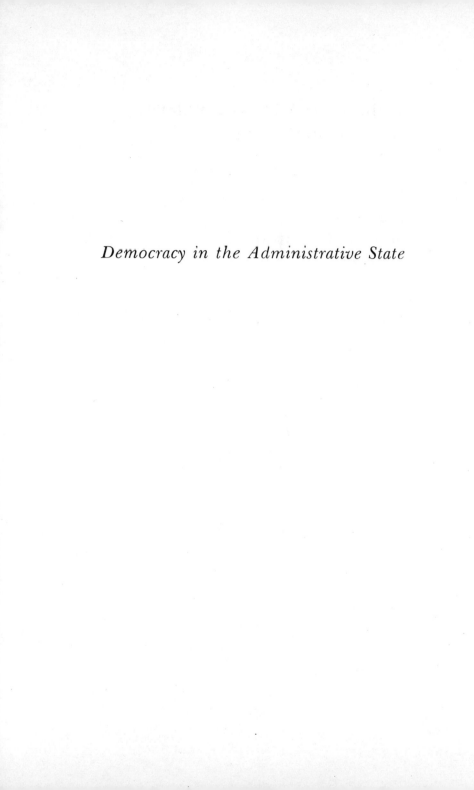

Democracy in the Administrative State

PUBLIC ADMINISTRATION AND DEMOCRACY

SERIES EDITOR   ROSCOE C. MARTIN

PUBLISHED

FREDERICK C. MOSHER
Democracy and the Public Service

OTHER VOLUMES ARE IN PREPARATION

Democracy in
the Administrative State

EMMETTE S. REDFORD

Ashbel Smith Professor of Government
The University of Texas at Austin

New York
Oxford University Press
London   Toronto   1969

Preface

BOTH normative concepts of democracy and empirical findings on the extent and limits of democracy in the United States are richly presented in postwar literature. Yet the potentialities for democracy where decisions are made and carried out through administrative institutions have not been examined. The purpose of this book is to initiate a discussion of this complex subject.

The span of the book is broad. The result inevitably is a lack of completeness in analysis of all the aspects of the subject on which suggestive comments are made. Of necessity, I cite only selectively from the vast literature that bears on the topics discussed. The objective has been to seek new insights into the areas where democracy and administration converge or overlap and to correlate our knowledge relating to democracy in the administrative state.

My debts are large. Dean Stephen K. Bailey gave me the opportunity to lecture, in collaboration with Professor Roscoe C. Martin, in the course on public administration and democracy at Syracuse University in the summers of 1965 and 1967. The University of Texas granted me leave for a semester to write this book. Professor Martin co-operated in the development of the project and offered many suggestions for improvement of the manuscript. The manuscript was also read by my colleague, Professor Orion F. White, Jr., and by my research assistant, Marlan J. Blissett—now visiting As-

v

sistant Professor at the University of Nebraska. Chapters were read also by other colleagues: Professors Murray C. Havens, Robert L. Lineberry, and Benjamin F. Wright. To each of these who have so generously helped in the development and improvement of this book I am grateful, but I cannot and would not shift blame onto them for inadequacies and imperfections that still remain.

Austin, Texas   *E. S. R.*
Fall 1968

Foreword

THIS IS the second volume in a projected series on the general subject of public administration and democracy. The first, Frederick C. Mosher's *Democracy and the Public Service*, was published in 1968. A third book, by Professor Dwight Waldo of Syracuse University, and a fourth, by Professor York Willbern of Indiana University, have been scheduled for publication; others will be announced as arrangements are completed.

In the volume at hand Professor Redford goes to the very heart of the concern of the whole series, whose purpose is to reconcile the practice of effective democracy with the positive and energetic public administration required by the modern state. The choice of the topic to be explored, the selection of its several aspects to be treated, and the sympathetic yet critical analysis which characterizes the book all testify to the author's deep understanding and firm grasp of the fundamental dilemmas to which the series as a whole is addressed.

Those concerned with the subject and acquainted with the author and his work will agree that Professor Redford is one of the handful of American scholars qualified to dissect democracy in the administrative state. His philosophical approach to public problems, his experience as a public administrator, and his renown as a scholar combine to equip him uniquely for the excursion he has undertaken here.

There may be those who will aver that Professor Redford has labored in behalf of a lost (or losing) cause. Democracy is a failure, some critics say, not least because of the pervasive and top-heavy administrative machinery it has fostered. The author knows well this point of view and indeed devotes much of his attention, by implication at least, to its refutation. To him democracy is neither dead nor dying, though he finds some merit in the complaints currently heard. What is required for the strengthening of American democracy is not the new start proposed by the disenchanted but rather the kind of cool-headed analysis of existing institutions and practices offered here. In *Democracy in the Administrative State,* Professor Redford reveals himself as a practical idealist. This book is not the first significant service the author has rendered to democracy and public administration, though juxtaposing the two as it does it may well be the most important. Almost certainly it is the most timely.

ROSCOE C. MARTIN

Contents

Democracy in the Administrative State

I

Democratic Morality, Public Policy, and the Political System

WE LIVE in an administered society. Although not all aspects of our life are managed for us, *we are affected intimately and extensively by decisions in numerous organizations, public and private, allocating advantages and disadvantages to us.* Many of these organizations are created, sustained, or controlled by the political system to such an extent that we differentiate them by use of the word "public." Some of these public organizations have continuous responsibilities for assigned specific functions—such as education, welfare, or national defense. These we refer to as "administrative."

We have a three-faceted development that distinguishes the twentieth century from the eighteenth and nineteenth. There is, first, the organizational revolution in society, which has produced the many organizations whose decisions affect our lives; second, the expansion of the functions of government; and third, the allocation of continuing or recurring aspects of public functions to administrative structures. The central elements in the administered society may be summarized as follows:

The Organized Society	Business, Labor, Social, Public
Public Organization	Legislative, Executive, Judicial
Public Administration	Departments, Bureaus, Commissions

3

The public administrative structures are not autonomous. They are part of the political system and operate with directions, restraints, and influences of various kinds from the many components of the political system, such as the President, the Congress, and interested organizations outside the government. There is a political-administrative system in which administrative organizations continuously carry on activities assigned to or arrogated by them, but within limits and constraints imposed from the outside. Since, however, this political-administrative system operates on individuals directly through administrative institutions, we can use the concise term "the administrative state" to characterize it. This is a political-administrative system which focuses its controls and renders its services through administrative structures but includes also the interaction of political structures through which these are sustained, directed, and limited.

Observers will look at the administrative state in different ways. Some may think of it as a Frankenstein monster extracting too much of national resources and threatening people's liberties. Others may look at the services performed by it with concern that these be effectively rendered, and perhaps expanded. In this volume I shall juxtapose the behavior of the administrative state with the American ideal of democracy. My purpose in this book is to reconcile the two.

I propose to explore the existence (or nonexistence) and the possibilities for achievement of democracy through the operations of the administrative state and the influences upon it. First, the essence of *democratic morality* and the many quandaries of its implementation in public policy will be explained in Chapter I. In Chapter II, I shall discuss factors that concentrate or disperse influence in the operation of the administrative state, and in the following three chapters, the way the administrative state operates—in policy development and its application—in our national government. These discussions on participation in the development and application of administrative programs and policy will

be followed by two on man as the subject of administration
and man as worker in administration. In all of these chapters the discussion of normative standards contained in democratic morality and of practices inherent in administrative
government will be accompanied by suggestions of means
for correlating the two. A concluding chapter will view the
administrative state in perspective. I will ask: Why do we
have it? What has been shown about its intrinsic nature?
What are the prospects, not for perfect realization of democratic morality, but for *workable democracy*—that is, for
maximum attainment of democratic morality under the conditions that have given rise to the administrative state? [1]

BASIC TENETS OF DEMOCRATIC MORALITY

What is the subject of our concern when we write about
democracy? We must write mainly about processes, but only

1. The concept of workable democracy may be compared to that of workable
competition, introduced by Professor J. M. Clark and used to refer to the
amount and kind of competition possible in the economy structured in organizations. See Clark, "Toward a Concept of Workable Competition," *American
Economic Review*, Vol. XXX (June 1940), pp. 241–56. And compare Joan
Robinson, *The Economics of Imperfect Competition* (New York: The Macmillan Company, 1933) and E. H. Chamberlin, *The Theory of Monopolistic
Competition: A Reorientation of the Theory of Value* (Cambridge, Mass.:
Harvard University Press, 1933).

The concept of workable democracy may be compared with Robert A.
Dahl's attempt to find the conditions that maximize democracy and his
definition of "polyarchies" as political systems where these conditions exist to
a "relatively high degree." See his *A Preface to Democratic Theory* (Chicago:
University of Chicago Press, 1956), especially pp. 71 and 84.

Workable democracy will be limited democracy and the reader may conclude that it is far less than the ideal set in democratic morality. It will be
democracy only to the extent that it approximates the ideal. We must guard
against the fallacy appearing in some of our literature that redefines democracy in terms of what exists in practice in a particular political system. See,
for discussion of such tendencies toward redefinition, Graeme Duncan and
Steven Lukes, "The New Democracy," *Political Studies*, Vol. XI (June 1963),
pp. 156–77, reprinted in Charles A. McCoy and John Playford, *Apolitical
Politics: A Critique of Behavioralism* (New York: Thomas Y. Crowell Co.,
1967), pp. 160–84.

because these have relevance to extra-process assumptions about democracy. Much analysis in modern political science is concentrated on the viability of political processes and especially the capacity of such processes to control tensions among people and to bring about peaceful adjustment of their differences. Such analysis extends also to change through political processes, through either evolution or revolution. Both tension control and tension explosion may, however, move in democratic, oligarchic, or dictatorial directions. In discourse on democracy, their significance is derivative.

Derivative from what? From three ideals that, compounded, produce democratic morality. The basic ideal is that persons are the units of value in social arrangements. It holds—notwithstanding any contrary assumptions of divine will or natural order—that institutions, policies, and the behavior of men are to be judged by one principle: Man is, for man, the ultimate measure of all human values. This is the individualistic foundation of democratic morality. We shall refer to it as the ideal of individual realization. The second ideal is that all men have worth deserving social recognition. In democratic morality neither the superior endowment, nor the earned or accidental advantage, nor the vested position of some can justify inattention to other men's needs. This is the equalitarian component of democratic morality. The third ideal is that personal worth is most fully protected and enlarged by the action of those whose worth is assumed. Democratic morality posits that on all matters where social action is substituted for individual action, liberty exists only through *participation either in decision making or in control of leaders who make the decisions.* Universal participation is, therefore, the third component of democratic morality.

In democratic morality the first two of these ideas constitute the ultimate purpose—the freedom and opportunity of all men for personal development based on the assumption of dignity and worth inherent in each individual. Democratic morality has an egoistic center, but within a conditional framework of universality. That is, each man's development is important and is conditioned by the moral right of every other man. The two ideas together produce the notion of a humane society.

The participation idea also has ultimate qualities. First, it assumes that the individual—rather than any elite of wisdom, wealth, power, or asserted divine right—is the rightful judge of the purposes of his life and the means for their realization. Moreover, participation may itself be a precious realization of man's potentials in social life. But it is also of instrumental value, for it is the means of realizing the goals of a humane society.

The democratic morality is supported on this point by historical and contemporary observation. Those who rule over others feather their own nests and make bare the nests of others. They convert their advantages into prescriptive rights and transmit them to unborn generations as unearned privileges. They are often brutal and their positions of status humble those who are excluded. The researcher may find exceptions to these realities in benevolent leadership for limited periods, but there is no basis in experience for a belief that subjects of power can ensure their personal realization without direct or indirect participation in the power itself.[2]

2. There has been argument, supported by some empirical evidence, that ruling elites show more loyalty to democratic *processes* ("rules of the game" for a democratic society) than the masses. See, for example, Herbert McClosky, "Consensus and Ideology in American Politics," *The American Political Science Review*, Vol. LVIII (June 1964), pp. 361–82, and the literature cited in the article. It can, of course, be expected that political participants will have acquired more familiarity with the values of participative process than nonparticipants, and also more allegiance to such process—because, and precisely because, they may be expected to have benefited from that participation. But their acceptance of democratic processes in a society of uneven participation is no assurance that the outcomes of policy will be favorable to the nonparticipants. V. O. Key suggested the possibility that "any assessment of the vitality of a democratic system should rest on an examination of the outlook, the sense of purpose, and the beliefs of that sector [aristocratic] of society." "Public Opinion and the Decay of Democracy," *Virginia Quarterly Review*,

The democratic morality admits flexibility in techniques of participation. It requires, however, meaningful participation, and for this there are many essentials. Among these are (1) access to information, based on education, open government, free communication, and open discussion; (2) access, direct or indirect, to forums of decision; (3) ability to open any issue to public discussion; (4) ability to assert one's claims without fear of coercive retaliation; and (5) consideration of all claims asserted. We call a society in which these conditions exist an open society, and democratic morality posits the open society as a precondition for attaining the humane society.[3]

Democratic morality will be meaningful only if it becomes part of the "received ideals" and the dominant spirit of a society. There must be acceptance of the conditions for a humane and open society: acceptance of the right of each to self-realization and to participation as means of self-realization. The first requires empathy, the second tolerance. These are "virtues" inherent in democratic morality. Moreover, democratic morality will be meaningful only if processes exist through which each person, with tolerance of the same opportunity for others, has opportunity for meaningful participation.

The bases of democratic morality lie deep in our culture. Visions of the humane society are offered in the Greek-Hebraic-Christian-Stoic tradition and expressed in this coun-

---

Vol. 37 (Autumn 1961), p. 491. But tolerance and benevolence in aristocratic groups, while perhaps assuring the stability and viability of the political system, cannot be expected, without the constraiｎ s of wider participation, to produce policy outcomes which accord with the equalitarian component of democratic morality.

3. In Robert E. Agger, Daniel Goldrich, and Bert E. Swanson, *The Rulers and the Ruled* (New York: John Wiley & Sons, Inc., 1964), "Developed Democracy" is defined as a "regime" in which there is a high "sense of electoral potency" and a low "possibility of illegitimate sanctions [e.g. loss of employment and extreme social ostracism] blocking efforts to shift the scope of government" (pp. 83ff.).

try in the Declaration of Independence. The ideal of participation is stated supremely in Aristotle's definition of a citizen in Book III of his *Politics.* He saw him as a man who is both ruler and ruled. The idea that this citizenship could be universal is our heritage from the nineteenth century. The twentieth century is, however, the time for discussion of the means of realizing the open society as the route to a humane society.

POLICY IMPLICATIONS AND QUANDARIES

Democratic morality produces many perplexing questions for those who think concernedly about public policy and its administration. Some of the policy implications and quandaries of democratic theory merit attention in this analysis.

Individual Realization

It is the democrat's hope that public policies will increase man's opportunities for self-development. By protecting men from restraints imposed by others, establishment of favorable conditions for individual development, and creation of social instruments continuously operating for humane purposes, collective action may give rise to individual opportunity for self-realization. Yet the first issue raising quandaries for the democrat is whether man's individuality will be suppressed rather than liberated, and his opportunity for self-development impaired rather than enlarged, by collective action. Will self-government exercised collectively destroy or impede individual self-development?

There are three factors that may simplify the problems of public policy presented by the first tenet of democratic morality. First, public policy is segmental. Although persons are the units of value, policy seldom deals with persons as such. It may do so, as when it protects life itself, e.g. in prohibiting murder; when it punishes through the death penalty; or when it seeks to rebuild the personality by mental treatment. But although clerics may seek the health of souls, psychiatrists the viable integration of personality, and totalitarians the subordination of man's will to social purpose, policy in open societies usually centers on assumed discrete requirements for personal development. Normally, the total fulfillment of man is too large and evasive for the aspirations of even the most sanguine policy maker, and the conditions under which policy is made in the open society focus attention on fragments of the forces affecting human development.

Related to this is the second factor: Policy does not usually relate to psychic realization but to men's actions and to external conditions believed to be required for human fulfillment. "Law," said Justice Frankfurter, "is concerned with external behavior and not with the inner life of man." [4] The most numerous policies of government have dealt with property, but always with the objective interests of men in property, not with a miser's or investor's satisfaction in counting his assets. When policy has sought to penetrate the inner consciousness, it has often been grossly ineffective. Law could, for example, prescribe forms of worship, but not the quality of spirituality that would emanate (or would not emanate) from it; nor could it curb the outbreak of other forms of spiritual expression. Speech could be restrained but not what a man thought; murder could be punished but not the contemplation of it. Modern welfare legislation, like property legislation, has been based on the assumption that material things are an essential for life, but such legislation has on the whole respected the personal life of the welfare recipient. A daily flag salute for school children designed to encourage patriotic sentiments was temporarily upheld by the Supreme Court but ultimately was struck down,[5] and

4. Dissenting in West Virginia State Board of Education v. Barnette, 319 U.S. 624 (1943). Many would say, however, that what Frankfurter was defending in this instance—namely, a flag salute—was an invasion of the inner life.
5. Minersville School District v. Gobitis, 310 U.S. 586 (1940), reversed in West Virginia State Board of Education v. Barnette, 319 U.S. 624 (1943).

affirmation of one's beliefs has been upheld only in narrow circumstances.[6]

Third, policy deals with requirements for personal realization that are shared by many persons. The basic essentials for life are shared generally, and the differentials required for quality realization by individuals are also shared by others. Thus, food is essential for all and art exhibits are required for those who share an interest in art. Inevitably, the policy maker's attention is attracted to shared needs and his time engaged in their consideration.

The shared needs are the discrete components of individual welfare with which viable policy deals. Policy outputs relate to objective, shared needs. We must, of course, be conscious of the intermingling of shared needs and of shared wants, attitudes, and demands—of objective and subjective connotations of the word "interest" which we use constantly in discussing policy formation and output. There are objective shared needs giving rise to interpersonal subjective attitudes; these latter, in turn, generate political demands (political inputs) that deal with objective, shared needs.

Whether viewed objectively as needs that collectively anticipate interpersonal subjective attitudes, or subjectively as shared attitudes that generate political demands, we relate shared interests to interest groups.[7] If they are shared generally or widely in a geographical entity—city, state, nation—they are often called public interests, and in the case of the nation some may be called national interests. Fortunately, much of the attention of policy makers is given to basic needs

---

6. See American Communications Association v. Douds, 339 U.S. 382 (1950).
7. For definition of "interests" as "shared attitudes" see David B. Truman, *The Governmental Process: Political Interests and Public Opinion* (New York: Alfred A. Knopf, 1962), p. 34. Truman cites sources for definition of "interests" as the "objects" toward which attitudes are directed: Robert M. MacIver, "Interests," *Encyclopaedia of the Social Sciences* (New York: The Macmillan Company, 1932), Vol. VIII, p. 147, and Avery Leiserson, *Administrative Regulation: A Study in Representation of Interests* (Chicago: University of Chicago Press, 1942), pp. 1–10.

shared generally by people in local or national communities.

In sum, the enormity of the first issue of democratic theory is materially reduced by the factors of selectivity, externality, and attentiveness to shared needs that are normally inherent in public policy making. This reduction does not, however, dispose of the problem, for certain quandaries of democratic theory remain.

There is, first, in contrast to selectivity, the factor of cumulation. Public policies may either foreclose or open much of man's opportunity for development of his potentials. This may be the result of single policies, as when man's status is defined as serf or slave. It may be the cumulative result of public policies that mesh with those of the private sector or, conversely, public policies that seek public management of the material and human resources of society, in either case enveloping many of the conditions that affect man's life. Selective, piecemeal policies may purposely enforce subjection upon groups of people—such as minorities of religion, race, or status. Or they may have a total effect beyond that contemplated or comprehended by the policy maker. This is the special quandary occasioned by the empirical policy response to conditions, which selects remedies for current situations but eschews attention to by-products of such policies and to the comprehensive and long-run effects of piecemeal policy interventions. This attention to the immediate is forced by pressures of groups seeking advantages and by limitations on human capacity to foresee long-run cumulative results.

There is, second, the quandary of socialization. Not all policy relates to externals. The largest domestic function of government in our day is education. Through education the minds of children and youth may be stereotyped in patterns fixed by the prevailing values of the society. And beyond the institutions of education, the minds of people are closed by the imposition of restrictions on communication of dissent. Hence, the democrat is faced with the possibility that the

socialization of individuals through education and the limitation of dissent may fix undemocratic patterns of thought.
He is faced also with the quandary as to how far the implementation of democratic morality requires consensus on
democratic values and how such consensus can be combined
with the ideal of an open society and of individual self-
realization. This problem of cultural co-operation versus
openness of individual development, heretofore thought of
in terms of limitations on disagreement—restrictions on free
speech, imposition of loyalty tests, and so on—now confronts
Americans in a new way as they seek to acculturate the Negro
and the poor to the dominant values of a middle-class society.

The protections for privacy may wither. Alan Westin's
recent book reveals the threats to man's privacy through new
instruments of surveillance wielded by organizations that
can accumulate data on his every activity from birth to death
and make it available to other organizations that can, perhaps operating secretly, punish or reward him in numerous
ways.[8] Lie detectors or other instruments may be means of
penetrating man's consciousness and opening new opportunities to those with totalitarian impulses. Social scientists
may learn how to direct our minds through education and
mass propaganda—indeed, even now the potentials for this
are frightening. Swarms of counsellors, armed with sanctions,
may seek to mold the lives of welfare recipients, and psychiatrists in various guises hover over all of us.

There are, finally, two qualifications of the sharing of interests that present quandaries for the democrat. The first is
the existence of conflicting interests. The interests shared by
some conflict with interests dear to others. The policy of
government necessarily reflects choices among interests. Some
men's interests as they conceive them will be overridden or
compromised in these choices. They may believe that their
opportunities for self-realization would be better achieved in

8. Alan F. Westin, *Privacy and Freedom* (New York: Atheneum, 1967).

the absence of public action of the type chosen by the policy maker. The other qualification is that policy must often be administered through particular applications. This creates practical problems: on the one hand, of avoiding unfairness and harshness to those who are subject to policy and, on the other, of avoiding differential advantages to those who are in a position to exert influence. In addition, there is the ever-present quandary of reconciling equal treatment of all in like circumstances with adaptations of policy to particular circumstances and to the particular requirements of individuals. These difficulties arising out of the nonsharing and unequal sharing of interests must receive further attention—immediately in the following subsection and repeatedly in the chapters that follow.

Equalitarianism

The quandaries of democratic theory produced by the tenet of equalitarianism are exceedingly complex and baffling. Basically, they arise out of the problem of minorities; yet the problem of minority interests is rarely analyzed in its various complexities.

There are, first, variations in kinds of satisfaction. One person likes to watch a football game, another to listen to a symphony; one likes to hunt and fish, another abhors such pursuits; one likes to be a participant, another is content with the role of spectator.

Quandaries resulting from differences in kind are increased by the possibility that there may be differences in quality. John Stuart Mill, seeking to correct the belief of earlier Utilitarians that every unit of happiness is equal to every other, observed that it is "better to be Socrates dissatisfied than a fool satisfied." This belief in the superiority of quality satisfactions is a bothersome one for democrats, for it can be used as the basis of argument for an aristocratic society. If there are qualitative differences in satisfaction, should not policy promote the opportunities of those with capacity for superior satisfactions? Should not society concentrate attention on developing its men of quality? Would not such a policy even have advantages for all men in society: first, to set a tone for the society and standards for attainment and, second, to provide leadership for the solution of society's problems?

There are answers for the democrat. First, he may suspect that policies for differential advantage of the few do not really create either superior satisfactions or leadership. Cocktails in café may produce no higher human satisfactions— even less genuine ones—than beer in the pub. The law in England that once protected the fox-hunting upper class by a death penalty for those who trespassed on hunting preserves shows only the excesses of social distinction, as does also the narrowness of a leadership class in Europe from whence could come the statement, "Let them eat cake." These excesses exhibit the false ring in bells molded by social distinction.

The democrat must, however, have more positive answers — and he does. First, there are basic uniform requirements for satisfactory living. Food and drink, shelter from the elements, health, education, and recreation are common needs. Moreover, there is probably within every healthy human being some capacity for appreciation of beauty and goodness. The payoff in personal satisfactions from public policy that provides the basic essentials for good living is undeniably high. For example, removal of causes of sickness or pain, or treatment of sickness, can add immeasurably to individual contentment. Hence, democratic morality has led to politics designed to secure for all the basic external conditions required for satisfactory living. Moreover, as a society becomes more affluent the levels of support for good living for all can be raised.

Second, quality satisfactions and quality leadership can be fostered in two ways that are consistent with democratic morality. One is for policy, in addition to providing basic essentials for meeting common needs, to encourage diversity for the benefit of those with uncommon qualities. For ex-

ample, educational policy can provide opportunity for re-
fined study in appreciative or creative art in its many forms
at the same time that it provides minimum levels of knowledge and appreciation. Or tax policy can allow deductions of
contributions to symphonies as well as deductions of those
to education. Choices between support for common and uncommon capacities may, of course, be necessary; but in an
affluent society the need for such choices will be reduced.

Another way democratic morality allows fostering of quality is by broadening the base from which quality may arise.
Lives of many great men show us that creativity, quality
leadership, and virtue may arise out of poverty, humble
position, and other circumstances of disadvantage. Yet talent
buried by lack of opportunity has been, and is, society's
greatest waste. For every person of talent who has had good
opportunity there must have been numerous others—even in
our own country—whose lives were stunted by unfavorable
circumstances. Democratic morality asserts this proposition:
Peaks of achievement will be most numerous in the society
that provides the greatest number of people with opportunities.

In addition to the problems arising from differences of
kind and quality are those fostered by differences of intensity. Intensity denotes degree. There are two aspects of it
that are significant in a discussion of democracy. First, intensity is a measure of internal gratification: the degree of
appreciation, for example, of the beauty of the sunset or the
message of the symphony. This is another aspect of quality,
and it may be promoted in the same ways that different kinds
of quality are promoted. Second, intensity varies in policy
preferences.[9] Some people may prefer a particular policy
much more than others. In this event, democratic theory

9. See, on this point, Robert A. Dahl, *A Preface to Democratic Theory,*
passim, particularly, pp. 48–50; V. O. Key, Jr., *Public Opinion and American
Democracy* (New York: Alfred A. Knopf, 1961), Chapter 9; and Willmoore
Kendall and George W. Carey, "The 'Intensity' Problem and Democratic
Theory," *The American Political Science Review,* Vol. LXII (March 1968),
pp. 5–24.

leaves the policy maker with no clear guides: votes and other quantitative measures cannot determine degree of intensity of preference.[10] Nor can the democrat answer positively to what extent such differences ought to be reflected in policy.

Another kind of difference is that in quantity of interest, that is, in the amount of stake one has in a matter. For example, assuming equality in all other factors, a mother with all of her five sons fighting in Vietnam has a greater stake in immediate peace than the mother whose sons are at home and past the age of draft call. The government worker who will get a 5 per cent increase in salary if a bill is passed in Congress has a greater quantity of interest in it than the person who does not work for the government.

Difference in quantity is different from difference in intensity of preference. Quantity is a measure of need, whereas intensity of preference is a purely internal reaction to what one perceives. The former is objective, the latter subjective. The two may or may not exist together. This is illustrated in the accompanying diagram. The mother of five sons in Vietnam, represented by A, has a high-quantity (objective) interest and is likely to have a high-intensity (subjective) interest; the apathetic Southern Negro, represented by B, has a high-quantity interest in many public policies but has low-intensity interest; the ardent advocate on ideological grounds of the abolition of capital punishment, represented by C, has a low-quantity interest and a high-intensity interest; and the consumer who does not travel, represented by D, has a low-quantity interest and low-intensity interest in wage negotiations in the airline industry.

10. After some experimentation with gross measures of opinion intensity, V. O. Key concluded that "the techniques for measuring intensity and the sparseness of the data limit our exploration of that trail. Intensity, one knows from offhand observation, varies over more steps than are suggested by the simple division of opinions into 'very strong' and 'not very strong.' Political concern runs from the most abject indifference through many gradations to an incandescence of interest shared by extremely few people." *Public Opinion and American Democracy*, p. 232. See also Kendall and Carey, "The 'Intensity' Problem and Democratic Theory," pp. 8–9.

Intensity of Preference

		High	Low
Quantity of Interest	High	A	B
	Low	C	D

Chart I   Intensity of Preference

It is surprising that this problem of differences in quantity of interest has received virtually no attention in the literature on democracy, particularly in view of politicians' consciousness of differences in quantity.[11] It is difference in quantity of interest that creates the toughest quandaries in the application of democratic theory to specific policy issues. The opportunities of men are not usually determined by sweeping decisions equally applicable to all, but grow out of policies affecting particular groups of men selectively and differently. And when as a result unequal amounts of interest exist for different persons, one cannot determine an issue merely by counting numbers. For example, when the wage of the worker in a factory is at issue, everyone in society has an interest as consumer of products; but the quantity of the interest of a given consumer is greatly inferior to that of the individual worker. The argument that consumers' interests should prevail over producers' interests falters when applied to *a particular situation*—when policies are made selectively for particular situations, numbers alone may not determine the equities.

It is not the problem of differences in internal gratification —of differences in units of happiness, as the Utilitarians dis-

11. For example, it is not mentioned in Lester W. Milbrath's perceptive analysis of factors influencing political participation. See his *Political Participation: How and Why People Get Involved in Politics* (Chicago: Rand McNally & Company, 1965). It receives minor attention in Charles E. Lindblom, *The Intelligence of Democracy: Decision Making Through Mutual Adjustment* (New York: The Free Press, 1965), especially pages 257–58 and 287ff.

cussed—that creates the toughest quandaries of democratic theory. It is rather the lack of a means for measuring equities where external factors related to men's realization of their purposes are being considered selectively by the policy maker. Public policy, I have said, deals usually with externals and with objective shared needs, and I can now add that seldom —if ever—does it relate to a simple situation in which there is equality of interest (objective need) among those affected.

The democratic morality supplies a general answer for the policy maker: the interest of every man has validity. But in the face of unequal quantities of interest, this answer is not a sufficient substantive standard. Moreover, the existence of unequal quantities of interest in particular situations compels attention to other processes of democracy besides majority rule.

Participation

Immediately, however, we must consider the third tenet of democratic morality—that of participation. Concerning this, there are three problems that demand our attention. The first is suggested by the question, who shall participate? It has usually been conceded that children, primitive people, and mental defectives should be excluded. This conclusion, though apparently unavoidable, must nevertheless bother the democrat.

While the love of parents for their children motivates interest in their welfare, the habit of elders of trying to stabilize the world, their concentration on meeting today's needs, and their failure to anticipate tomorrow's threats to a humane society, may foreclose or impair the opportunities of today's children to participate meaningfully tomorrow. One may look, for example, at today's actions, or lack of actions, with respect to such things as forest preservation, pollution of water and air, and subsidies for the shipping industry that cancel some options for the decision makers of tomorrow. Those who think of a planned world for tomorrow should

be concerned about what Edwin Bock calls the "new colonials"—men of the future whose interests are affected by
decisions of today.[12] Moreover, the democrat must be interested in whether the elders of today are providing all children with education that equips them for free and intelligent
participation in an open society.

There is, of course, the problem of age of admission to
participation. Participation in some forms of social decision
may be possible at an early age, and many persons now have
doubts about twenty-one as the age of attainment of responsible, intelligent judgment. Reduction of the voting age to
eighteen in some areas reflects this concern.

Benevolent trusteeship may be the best attainable arrange-
ment for mental defectives, but for a primitive people it
cannot be the ultimate answer for the democrat. The trusteeship position is a difficult one. It involves restraint on self-
interest of the policy maker that is difficult if not impossible
to achieve; difficult judgments on substitution of new modes
of life for old; and preparation of wards for their own self-
government and for timely termination of the trust.

The basic answer of democratic morality to this first question is that participation should be as wide as possible. Persons must not be excluded because they have no stake in the
existing order, for it is their stake in an opportunity for
realization that is at issue. Sex and race are irrelevant tests
for participation under democratic tenets. Ignorance is a
hazardous basis for exclusion: It can be assumed where it does
not exist, and any exclusion nullifies protection against those
who profess to have wisdom. Moreover, ignorance may be
correctable.

The second problem is scope of participation. While it
would seem that the fullest attainment of democratic morality would be realized if every person participated in all

12. See Edwin A. Bock, *The Last Colonialism: Governmental Problems Arising from the Use and Abuse of the Future* (CAG Occasional Papers, American Society for Public Administration, Bloomington, Indiana, 1967).

decisions that affected him—materially, at least—this is not possible when more than a few simple functions are performed by the state. No man could handle the information flow necessary to inform himself on all that affected him. Moreover, he could not organize with his fellows means of participating in all policy decisions. Consequently, the individual has two ways of participating. One is generalized participation, where he has a part in the selection of persons who presumably will represent his interests on the variety of matters on which decisions are made. This, however, is remote participation, for his delegation passes first to a representative and then often, in the administrative state, to other agents in departments, bureaus, and other centers of decision on specific policies.

The other is selective participation. From the inflow of information, a person receives signals on things on which he has intense preferences or quantity interests and as a consequence he may look for a means of participating on these. This participation may also be remote through levels of agents, though it may be more weighty because of a person's concentration of effort on it. Yet because such individual concentrations, when aggregated through group collaboration and use of channels of access to decisional forums, do increase the weight of participation, an imbalance in representation of interests may be created between those participating selectively and other persons, and imbalances may also be created among those participating selectively but with unequal influence. There is, in sum, an inegalitarianism inherent in selective participation.

Whether the inequality of influence in selective participation is contrary to democratic assumptions is difficult to judge because of the third problem with respect to participation. This is the problem of equating participation with quantity of interest. If there is validity in the assumption that in particular situations for which policy is made larger quantities of interest justify larger claims for attention, democratic morality will call for unequal participation—that is, unequal access in terms of numbers of people. We are brought back to the central quandary of democratic theory: How can distributed, low-quantity interests of the many and high-quantity interests of the few in particular policy confrontations be mediated? It may be possible for majoritarian impulses to destroy channels of individual realization, or conversely for aggregated, high-quantity interests of some people to prevail over other high-quantity interests or to override distributed interests to such an extent that, in a society of complex interrelationships, the capacities of some or even of all for self-realization are limited. To be specific, some of our number may be too lightly asked to die for the rest of us. Or in labor-management relations, the capacity for self-realization by either laborers or managers/investors may be impaired, or conversely the distributed interests of all people may be adversely affected by imbalances in access of groups representing the various divergent and concordant interests. In sum, in a pluralistic society the democratic morality runs full force into the problem of a balance in representation of interests of varied quantities.

ROUTES TO DEMOCRACY

This problem of balance points to need for discussion of ways of implementing democratic morality. Traditional literature has told us about three routes to democracy. In beginning a discussion of these routes I offer the hypothesis that all three are essential to approximation of or to progress toward democratic morality.

The first route is search for an implementation of consensus. This is the route offered by Rousseau in the concept of the general will. While critics have emphasized the indefiniteness, impracticability, and limitations of Rousseau's use of the concept, modern political science has given increasing recognition to the significance of consensus in the political system. Robert Dahl is emphatic, in language that may some-what overstate:

> In a sense what we ordinarily describe as democratic "politics" is merely the chaff. It is the surface manifesta-tion, representing superficial conflicts. Prior to politics, beneath it, enveloping it, restricting it, coordinating it, is the underlying consensus on policy that usually exists in the society among a predominant portion of the po-litically active members. . . . With such a consensus the disputes over policy alternatives are nearly always dis-putes over a set of alternatives that have already been winnowed down to those within the broad area of agreement.[13]

If the society is one in which political activity is generally and effectively open to all mentally competent adults, then embodiment of the consensus into public policy is instru mentalization of democratic morality. We need, of course, to be conscious of several facts: first, that the "predominant portion" may not be everybody—dissenters, in fact, may be numerous and have high-intensity preferences or high-quan-tity interests; second, that the politically active may not be a representative portion of the community; and third, that this creates problems of liberty and due process for the dis-senter and of representation for those who are currently ex-cluded from or are inactive in the political process. We need also to recognize that this is not the whole route—that before policy is made operational, decisions will most always have to be made with respect to areas of disagreement. But policy makers—political and administrative leaders and policy ana-lysts—can function toward democratic morality when they are knowledgeable about the consensus in their society and imaginative in developing policies that respond to, or even expand, the consensus.

The elements of consensus—based on shared ideals and

13. Robert A. Dahl, *A Preface to Democratic Theory*, pp. 132–33.

interests—in American society undoubtedly supply some broad guides for policy making. The consensus is a moving one, growing as policy evolves and as leadership is exercised successfully. One could define, for example, new elements of wide consensus evolving after the New Deal legislation (e.g. on collective bargaining, social security, regulation of security issues) or after the Supreme Court decisions against discrimination in transportation, voting in primaries, and public education.[14]

The second route is majority determination. Majoritarianism is sometimes seen as the kernel of Lockean or Jeffersonian political philosophy, but neither advocate was a strict majoritarian. Dahl has summarized fully the substantial ethical, technical, and empirical limitations on majoritarianism which militate against its unqualified acceptance.[15] I have discussed some of the ethical quandaries, and have emphasized particularly the ethical and practical quandaries presented by the existence of unequal quantities of interest. I need here only mention some of the technical limitations in order to illustrate their significance: the usual inability to offer single policy issues for vote of the electorate, the limitation even then on the alternatives that can be submitted, the frequent failure to obtain a majority for one if more than two alternatives are submitted, and the failure to get participation of all whose interests are affected. Even when the people vote on representatives, their options are limited, and if more than two options are presented a majority may not be obtained for any representative.

Nevertheless, majority expression is one route to democracy. First, sensitive policy makers may often know that a majority favors a policy, just as they may know that there is

14. An example of legislation on the basis of a broad consensus, rather than of bargaining or of choice among contending claims, is provided in my analysis of the passage of the Civil Aeronautics Act of 1938. "The Significance of Belief Patterns in Economic Regulation," *The Western Political Quarterly,* Vol. XIV (September 1961), pp. 13–25.

15. Dahl, *A Preface to Democratic Theory,* pp. 38–44.

a preponderance that is sufficient to be called a consensus.[16] Polling can help to validate this sensitivity. While differences in intensity of preference or in quantities of interest may often leave doubts as to the ethical validity of majority determination of an issue, it is still true that the majority determination will deserve attention. Second, in the many forums in which policy is decided, there is often no practicable alternative to some form of majority judgment—either a simple majority, an extraordinary majority, or concurrent majorities. Third, while the majority expression of the populace may rarely be determinative of particular policy issues, it is an essential device for control of the leaders whose decisions will determine policy.

The third route to democratic morality is consideration of the requirements in policy to satisfy differences in kind, quality, intensity, and quantity of interest. There are three general reasons why this third route is essential for realization of democratic purpose. The first is that individuals in minorities retain under democratic morality the moral claim to an opportunity for self-development. This may require protection against majority will. Or it may require promotion of opportunities for realizations that are different in kind and quality from those desired by the majority. We can note, for example, the problem of giving to the different groups of television viewers programs that are adjusted to their various tastes.

The second reason is the enormous variation in quantities of interest in a complex society, particularly an industrialized society that creates numerous employments requiring different talents in different amounts. Insofar as it is possible to

16. On the importance of a congressman's perceptions in linking constituency attitudes and his policy decisions, see Warren E. Miller and Donald E. Stokes, "Constituency Influence in Congress," *The American Political Science Review*, Vol. LVII (March 1963), pp. 45–56, and Charles F. Cnudde and Donald J. McCrone, "The Linkage between Constituency Attitudes and Congressional Voting Behavior: A Causal Model," *The American Political Science Review*, Vol. LX (March 1966), pp. 66–72.

gain consensus for policies of broad effect that enhance the opportunities of each person for employment of the kind he wants with the renumeration he finds satisfactory, the problem of quantity variations may be escaped. When, on the other hand, policies are particularized for separate industries or types or location of employment, the differences in the quantities of interest cannot be avoided by the policy maker.

The third reason carries us beyond themes heretofore analyzed. It is that *policy is indeed made for situations in which there is a web of conflicting, concurring, and intermingling interests of different kind, quality, intensity, and quantity.* This being true, decision solely on the basis of numbers of persons affected favorably or unfavorably would be a clumsy approach to solution of problems. Such decisions might be inexpedient in that failure to consider the high-quantity interests of the active persons in the situational web could inhibit their initiatives and thus impair the operation of the economy or the well-being of the society. They would, also, if my previous analysis is correct, distort the effort to realize democratic purpose by counting unequal quantities of interest as equal.

Three propositions may be derived from this analysis. First, when consensus or majoritarianism are not the exclusive routes to decision, access of each interest to be materially affected by a decision to the forum in which the decision is made is the only means of participation that can satisfy democratic tenets. There are elements of inconclusiveness in this proposition: Access in what sense: merely as avenue of approach or as capacity to coerce the decision maker to consideration or action? Equal access or access proportional to quantity of interest? But the core of the proposition is that distinct interests cannot be protected without meaningful opportunity for their assertion. This proposition is merely an expansion of the principle of representation, which becomes a device not only for registering consensus or majority wishes but also for obtaining consideration of numerous variations in interest.

The second proposition is that democratic policy making extends beyond search for consensus and majority expression to the brokerage of various interests. Perhaps the greatest advance in modern political science is increasing discernment about this approach to democracy—albeit at times with underemphasis on the two other routes. The idea has its basis in the kind of political thought offered by Madison, but I think the threshold was crossed in contemporary analysis in Pendleton Herring's substantiation by case analyses of the reconciliation theory in 1936.[17] The theory is that policy is made by balancing claims of interest and mediating among them. The empirical values of mediation are often stated: primarily that successful mediation ensures stability in policy and reduces tensions in society. But it is also defended, and I think correctly, as a means of implementing democratic morality.

The third proposition is that brokerage itself is a complex process of compromise, choice, and search for consensus. The policy maker may try pure compromise—two measures of benefit to one group, two to the opposing, and perhaps one to others. He will also have to make choices. Yet to overcome the insecurity of pure compromise, and to avoid the necessity of choices, he will seek enlargement of the perceptions of agreement in interest among contending parties. The resolution of differences is made possible and stabilized by appeal to shared values. William Gore has said, "The consensus generated around simple values is the *penultimate condition of all effective organizational action.*" [18] It is, I am saying here, a regular part of the process of mediation and the most secure base for stable solutions.

In sum, we can think of the routes to democracy in terms of a model of three parallel tracks on which the policy maker travels—often in alternation, or with retractable wheels rest-

17. E. Pendleton Herring, *Public Administration and the Public Interest* (New York: McGraw-Hill Book Co., Inc., 1936).
18. William J. Gore, *Administrative Decision—A Heuristic Model* (New York: John Wiley & Sons, Inc., 1964), p. 82.

ing with uneven weight on two or all three tracks. He moves his vehicle as far as he can on the smooth track of consensus; he changes as necessary to the rough track of reconciliation of conflict; he rides farther with a wheel on each, seeking reconciliation by compromise and further development of consensus; and he rides occasionally on the majoritarian track, either by gauging the interests affected or by sharing the decision power with others, and hopes that he finally may travel again on the smooth track of a newly developed consensus. The sequences and combinations will vary, but all three tracks are used; and this analysis of the quandaries of democratic theory supports the hypothesis that all three are essential routes to democracy.

The complexities of making policy in line with democratic morality present us with some important consequences. First, we are left without quantitative measures of the consonance between policies and democratic morality. Consensus and majority are quantitative terms, but they do not offer the policy maker, or the policy evaluator, absolute quantitative answers. The degree of preponderance of opinion that can be assumed as the measure of consensus cannot be stated categorically in percentages. The validity of a majority count will for both technical and ethical reasons often be uncertain. When reconciliation is the method, then there is nothing to gauge except the degree of consensus, which is certainly not quantitatively measurable. It is gaugeable only by the extent of objection or acceptance of those in affected groups who have capacity and will to express objection or acceptance in ways that can be heard. One particular difficulty is determining the time at which consensus should be gauged—many decisions are immediately the subject of controversy but ultimately are almost universally accepted, or vice versa. If one turns from results to processes he discerns the difficulty, or impossibility, of gauging conclusively whether the consensus, majority, or reconciliation was achieved by the proper balances of influences, with equal claims gaining equal consideration, unequal claims receiving appropriate attention, and the two being correctly balanced. Quantitative methods may help, but they cannot determine judgments on achievement of democratic morality.

Second, while the perfection of processes cannot be quantitatively gauged, the basic assurance of democratic morality will be process that provides multiple and universal access to decision-making forums. The importance of access for each interest has already been noted, but it is desirable to stress the requirement of multiple and diverse access for achievement of democratic ideals. Election of representatives, or referendums on issues, have always been recognized as key means of access. But more participation than this will be necessary to implement democratic morality in an administered society. Group organization and pressures, presentation of expert opinion, wide discussion, demonstrations, and perhaps even some civil disobedience are among the many methods that may be required for meaningful access. It should be added that access is meaningful only if it has a sufficiently coercive quality to ensure consideration of claims presented.

Third, in the decision-making process the *forums of decision making* that constitute the structure of the administrative state and in which access is pinpointed are crucial to the realization of the democratic ideal. Decisions are made by interactions within and among institutions. These institutions are themselves means of access—that is, interests are represented *in and by the operation of institutions,* as well as *before* institutions. The Framers of the Constitution assumed that representation of different interests would be carried into the forums of decision. "And what," said Madison, "are the different classes of legislators but advocates and parties to the causes which they determine?" [19] Decisions on administrative organization reflect the expectation that cer-

19. *The Federalist,* No. 10 (Wright, ed., Cambridge, Mass.: Harvard University Press, 1961).

tain kinds of interest will be promoted by the kind of organization chosen. Specifically, decisions on whether to have a
commission or a single-headed agency for economic regulation, or on qualifications of heads of agencies, reflect the
choices of decision makers on interests to be promoted. Every
forum of decision ultimately comes to represent in its purpose, in the rules and policies it follows, and in the roles of
its personnel, some combination of interests. There is no
such thing as a neutral decision on these matters—even the
decision to have a presumably neutral agency is a decision
that certain interests shall prevail.

Organizations constituting the administrative state are,
therefore, representational—that is to say, they have positions with respect to interests. Moreover, the forums have
continuity. They are instruments through which interests can
get continuing representation and in which new interests may
seek representation. Finally, they come to have a weight of
their own in decision making. This may have been intended
by their creators, but it may also be unforeseen or unin-
tended. The weight of forums accrues from the interests they
represent and from the strategic position they occupy in
decision-making processes.

It follows from what has been said that realization of
democratic morality is dependent upon *processes through
which interests obtain meaningful access to or into forums*
in which policies are made and translated into action. Access
is offered by institutions forming a political system, and some
of these are the continuing institutions we call administrative. These administrative institutions *and their relationships
with the rest of the political system* have been referred to in
the title of this book as "the administrative state." It is not
possible today to discuss democracy meaningfully without
attention to these administrative institutions, but these in
turn cannot be discussed meaningfully without attention to
the total political system of which they are a part. I shall in
the succeeding chapters concentrate attention on our ad-

ministrative institutions as part of the total political system through which policy decisions are made and applied, and shall consider the relevance of these institutions and their functioning to the realization of democratic morality.

DEMOCRATIC MORALITY AND THE POLITICAL SYSTEM

Before embarking on this adventure, however, another aspect of democratic morality should be analyzed, namely its relation to other purposes of the political system. Two tests of a political system, besides those inherent in the democratic ideal, open up additional quandaries of democratic theory.

One test is the wisdom of policies. Plato gives us an ancient model of a good political system. He begins with a quest for a definition of justice and offers what in modern terms could be called an efficiency model—one in which each person makes the contribution to the society for which he is best equipped. The function of policy making is that of the wise men. The wise men are an elite distinct from other groups and responsive in no way to expressions of the will of other groups.

Wisdom, or the knowledge required for it, is highly functionalized in modern society. Hence, wisdom in policy making is not attainable without the participation of specialized experts. Any modern version of the Platonic model would include men of science, diplomacy, medicine, and education in the category of men of wisdom determining scientific, diplomatic, health, and educational policies, respectively.

The men with specialized knowledge, in addition to developing concepts and theories to explain reality, search for wise policies in the areas in which they are proficient. Thus, for example, economists try to provide us with wise answers on economic policy. The assumption is that men ought to want policies that operate beneficently toward human goals and that the standards for attainment of this objective will derive from the knowledge of the specialists. The political system, in turn, will be a good one if it embodies this knowledge in policy.

What is the response from democratic theory? I think it lies in two general propositions and three subsidiary rules. The first proposition is this: There is nothing in democratic morality that excludes the use of specialized knowledge in policy-making forums. The democrat should welcome the wisdom of the experts because without it his goal of human attainment cannot be realized. The creative expert is an essential contributor to the attainment of democratic purpose.[20] Second, democratic morality asserts that responsiveness to the people's will is the ultimate test of public policy. It rejects the right of any elite to *impose* its will. For example, it can accept the right of medical experts to inform the people on the effects of smoking but not the right of the experts to prescribe a rule that no one shall smoke. What this adds up to in effect is this: first, the ultimate test of policy must be the political test, that is, the will of the people affected by the policy and, second, this will must be reflected in processes that accord with the participative tenet of democratic morality.

The rules derivable from democratic morality are these: First, the expert must offer his wisdom to society for its verdict. The issues of policy must be opened to discussion. This does not mean that leadership from elites is excluded; it means, rather, that the leaders must supply an informed discussion. The second rule is that time should be provided for adequate testing of the proposals of experts in the forums of opinion. The third rule is that the discussion must be free and open.

There are, therefore, potential means of reconciling the claims for wisdom and those for responsiveness as goals of a

---

20. I have elaborated this argument in my *Administration of National Economic Control* (New York: The Macmillan Company, 1952), pp. 228–33, and *Ideal and Practice in Public Administration* (University, Alabama: University of Alabama Press, 1958), pp. 130–35.

political system. The hazards are, however, great. One is that the gap between the wisdom of the experts and that of men in the mass may be so large that it cannot be bridged by discussion. Some others are that, particularly in the expanding area of international affairs, men of knowledge may assert the necessity of secrecy; that in periods of emergency, decisions that irrevocably commit the society may be made without allowance of time for discussion; that disagreements among experts will be concealed; and that discussion will be distorted by biases in communication channels. There are, in addition, other impediments to democratic consideration that will appear in the next chapter.

Contemporary political science has offered another test of a political system. I referred to it at the beginning of this chapter. It is the capacity of the political system to control tensions. A political system is regarded as having a meritorious quality if the claims of groups can be moderated, absorbed, and adjusted within it by nonviolent processes. Peaceful brokerage of claims and the stability and continuity of the political system through which this is made possible are the values by which a political system is tested. Charles E. Lindblom has written, "Most of us in the Western tradition would, if faced with a practical choice, probably sanction any degree of inequality necessary to maintain a government based on consent rather than a high degree of repression." [21]

Experience under the American political system is often used to illustrate these values. In a nation of diversity and often of deep conflict, the tensions between sections and groups have been resolved through peaceful processes through most of our history. There was one terrible failure when sectional division in the nation was excised through four years of "blood and iron." But for more than a full century since the Civil War the processes of peaceful adjustment have operated successfully, though placed under strain by such things as labor-management conflict over a period of years and racial tensions in recent years.

21. Lindblom, *The Intelligence of Democracy*, p. 260.

What is the response to the tension-control test from democratic theory? On the one hand the democrat will accept tension control as one aspect of democratic purpose. Peace may be a more secure route to human achievement than violent conflict, as the histories of England since 1688 and of the United States since 1783 evidence. Also, reconciliation of varied claims, which has been set forth as one route to democracy, is facilitated by tension control. But on the other hand the democrat will view tension control as an insufficiently comprehensive test of a political system. He will see in it a possible bias toward stability and continuity of the political system and hence against assertions of claims that threaten the stability of the existing order. In other words, he will identify a bias toward the status quo and the interests protected by it.

The exponents of the tension-control test may respond by saying that a political system could not continuously maintain an adjustment of interests if it did not respond to new claims asserted by groups rising to power. The merit of the American system, it would be asserted, has been its ability to broaden its responses to new claims upon it in a society of rapid change. At the same time, however, the idea has been suggested that inactivity of groups whose claims have not been accommodated in the past may be an advantage because it does not threaten the stability of the political system.[22] This view out of learned literature would be acceptable to a southerner placing high value on the durability of his po-

---

22. The suggestion may have its origins in Bernard R. Berelson, et al., *Voting: A Study of Opinion Formation in a Presidential Campaign* (Chicago: University of Chicago Press, 1954), Chapter 14. "How could a mass democracy work if all the people were deeply involved in politics? Lack of interest by some people is not without its benefits, too. . . ." (p. 314). The suggestion is explicit or implicit in other literature. For argument over the intent and significance of the comments interpretable as embodying the suggestion, see Jack L. Walker, "A Critique of the Elitist Theory of Democracy," *The American Political Science Review*, Vol. LX (June 1966), pp. 285–95; Robert A. Dahl, "Further Reflections on 'The Elitist Theory of Democracy,'" ibid. pp. 296–305; and Walker's rejoinder, ibid. pp. 391–92.

litical system and low value on its accommodation of all group interests, specifically those of the Negro population.

The view would not be acceptable to the democrat. He would want to know whether the political system was an open one that provided ability to all men in society to obtain meaningful access to forums in which the interests of all would be considered. He would recognize that a political system could accommodate the interests of the politically powerful sufficiently to maintain itself and control tensions over a period of time and that it would not provide meaningful access to large portions, or even a majority, of its citizens.[23]

Under the democratic morality, neither wisdom as judged by an elite (or set of elites) nor tension-control by itself is the ultimate test of the moral claims of a political system. The ultimate test is the responsiveness of the system to the views of the people within its jurisdiction—responsiveness resulting from the people's participation, either in policy making or through control of those who make policy.

This test may produce quandaries for the democrat in particular situations. Shall he, because of apparent necessity or the imperfections in implementation of democratic morality, accept decision making by those who presumably have access to facts and intelligence for judgment based on those facts, even if the decision is irrevocable or cannot be openly and fully evaluated? In sum, does democratic morality allow delegations of final judgment to men of wisdom? And can the democrat accept tension control and continuity of the political system as values even though they limit the immediate realization of democratic goals? How shall he balance, for example, the values of the maintenance of a system of law and order against the violent assertion of claims by those who believe they have no meaningful access to the system?

23. The best of the two worlds may be assumed in an argument that in a world of change consent is maintainable only in a democratic society. See, for an example, Philip E. Slater and Warren G. Bennis, "Democracy Is Inevitable," *Harvard Business Review*, Vol. XLII (March 1964), pp. 51–59.

Is violence itself a democratic instrument under certain conditions? And if he accepts any delegation to the men of wisdom and the men of order, will he not realize that he is accepting delegations to men of power—a perpetuation of imbalances in power positions irreconcilable with democratic theory?

A political system is a complex thing representing multiple values. The democrat will assert that responsiveness is its ultimate test and will hope that wisdom, together with continuity through tension control, can be achieved through it. But he will be left with quandaries and may find that his democratic morality is compromised by necessity or by admission of other values into his own morality.

SUMMARY

Democratic morality rests on three tenets: individual realization, equality of men in their claims for attention, and participation—either directly or through control of leaders —as the instrument of implementation of substantive values. This morality leaves many quandaries in the practical world of policy making. With respect to the first tenet, the enormity of the quandaries is reduced (but not eliminated) by the tendencies of policy to deal with *external* conditions affecting *some* needs *shared by groups* of men. With respect to the second, the quandaries remain because of the differences in kind, quality, and quantity of objective interests and in the subjective reflection of these in different intensities of preference. The quandaries are only partially reduced by opportunities for policy to deal both with uniformities and diversities. The quandaries can be met partially by concurrent routes toward implementation—search for consensus, majority decision, and reconciliation of claims. Regarding the third tenet, there are quandaries about who should be admitted to participation and how selective and unequal participation, particularly when high-quantity interests are involved, can be reconciled with democratic morality. In addition, there are quandaries because of confrontation of democratic morality with other tests of a political system. Responsiveness is the central theme of democratic morality, but wisdom, and tranquility and order, are competing claims of political purpose.

II

—————

Reflections on the Administrative State

THE PRECEDING CHAPTER dealt with democratic morality and with the quandaries either inherent in it or arising from its competition with other ideals. I believe that in spite of the quandaries, most Americans accept democratic morality as part of the core of purpose they desire to be reflected in the policies of the political system. This chapter emphasizes some pertinent realities of the world we live in. It seeks answers to these questions: What is natural, regular, and persistent in the operations of our public administrative institutions? What are the implications of these factors for realization of the democratic ideal? In facing these questions, attention will be focused on the facts that concentrate or disperse influences in and on functioning administrative organizations that serve or control us. I seek to place in juxtaposition the democratic ideal and the policy-making process in the administrative state.

INSTITUTIONAL FEATURES

The essence of the administrative state is that men are born and live not merely, as Rousseau said, in subordination to power, but under a regime in which they are both served and controlled by an institutional complex composed of organizations. Their political society is structured in organizational systems and subsystems. These may lack rigidity—may, in fact, be subjected to additions, alterations, and terminations—but the qualities of the administrative state in a given cultural context remain relatively constant.

Structural Specialization

The basic feature of the administrative state is its structural specialization. The affairs administered for us are assigned to organizations with specialized functions.

We have distinguished these functional allocations in various ways. Thus we have distinguished legislative, executive, and judicial functions. Again, we have distinguished between policy-making, directing and controlling structure, and operating or executing structure. Within public administrative organizations we have differentiated four types of allocation: by area (as between home office and field office, or between national and state units of administration), by process (as budgeting, accounting, personnel work, scientific research), by clientele served (as veterans, Indians), or by purpose or program (as education, national defense, health). In the case of any of these classifications, the lines between categories often are blurred in the allocation of duties to organizations. Legislative and executive functions may be commingled in the same organizations, policy making and policy execution fused at a given level of organization, and different types of allocation—area, process, clientele, and purpose—mixed in the same organization.[1]

Particularly significant, however, is the way organization develops in response to purpose, i.e. substantive function to be performed. Our administrative structure—i.e. our arrangements for continuing service or control—develops in clusters of organizations for such discrete functions as edu-

1. See Luther Gulick, "Notes on the Theory of Organization," in L. Gulick and L. Urwick, eds., *Papers on the Science of Administration* (New York: Institute of Public Administration, 1937), pp. 15–31.

cation, health, national defense, conservation of resources. Let us look for a moment at the bridges spanned by this *program functionalization*. First, we shall see in Chapters III and IV the extent to which the separation of powers in the national government has been broken down by the concurrent activities of legislative and executive units of organization dealing with particular functions, and that even the process distinctions between legislation and administration are obscured. Second, if there were any doubt previously, Morton Grodzins and Daniel Elazar have now shown that the division of powers among national, state, and local governments has long been tempered by joint participation in particular functions by two or more levels of government.[2] Third, the boundaries between public and private jurisdictions are being bridged and obscured by correlation of the activities of the two in such diverse fields as production for national defense, nuclear energy development, housing, health, and education. One finds in each of these areas public and private institutions contributing toward the particular purpose.

Significant also is the extent to which *the continuing business of society is in commission to organizations with program specializations*. The old view that all important policy decisions could be made by legislatures and that specialized organizations would be "administrative" only is no longer tenable, if indeed it ever was. First, specialized organizations have been delegated, or they have assumed, responsibility for making policy decisions with respect to their programs. Second, they contain within them program specialists who will inform society about their programs, propose alterations in policy, and influence decisions by voters and their representatives. Finally, they create and aggregate interests clustered around and in the organizations—interests supported

2. For the final fruits of their research, see Morton Grodzins (Daniel J. Elazar, ed.), *The American System: A New View of Government in the United States* (Chicago: Rand McNally & Company, 1966), particularly Part II.

by survival and expansion of their functions. They enlarge
the weight of these interests in policy making. The interests
may be sufficiently large and congruent to create a community of interests with a strong position with respect to a
particular function. This is what President Eisenhower feared
when he warned in his farewell address of an industrial-
military complex. But with varying degrees of concentration
in organization and unity of interests, we have functional
complexes of interrelated interests in every program area,
such as education, law enforcement, highway construction,
and agricultural stabilization.

How can the variety of interests be protected and promoted
in a society of administrative complexes? One answer is division within the complexes. This answer is reflected in antitrust policy for the private sector and in separation of powers,
federalism, and administrative fragmentation in the public
sector. Its efficacy is threatened by concentrations in both
private and public sectors. In some arenas of public policy—
such as defense, diplomacy, and space exploration—concentrations may be inevitable. Moreover, there is no assurance
that mere division produces representation of all interests.
For example, fifty or three thousand complexes can be as
oblivious to the interests of minorities as one. A second
answer is the traditional one of overhead democracy, which
is that the voter's representatives in legislative and executive
positions will direct and control administrative organizations. A third answer is direct access of diverse interests to the
functional organizations to which policy making is delegated.

Strategic Positions
I shall return repeatedly to the latter two answers, but here
let us consider another institutional feature. Influence on
decisions gets allocated to positions within organizations,
which I shall refer to as *strategic positions (or locations)*.

Not every one in organizations has equal influence on decisions. Some gain a place of greater influence by (1) formal

delegation of authority to the position they hold, (2) practice within the organization affecting potential influence of positions, or (3) technical competence or personal qualities that give them special status. Strategic positions may, therefore, be created by formal allocation of duty and status or by developments within an organization that effectively allocate influence. The presidency is a strategic location. So, also, is the headship of a department, the chairmanship of a congressional committee, or the presidency of a trade association. Formal establishment of these positions creates potential for influence, which almost certainly results in real influence. But included within strategic positions are also the professionals—men with specialized knowledge and experience who because of positions they have acquired are able to contribute information, counsel, and judgment to organizational decisions. The point I seek to make is that policy making is achieved by focusing the action of men through strategic positions in organizations.

This concept ascribes more concentration of influence at the focal points of policy making than is asserted in the concepts of minority rule and program specialization. Policy making is concentrated in *minorities within specialized structures*. The concept does not, of course, tell the whole story. Men at strategic centers are impelled and restrained from outside, first by the access of individuals and groups to their positions, and second by the broader forums (Congress, public opinion, etc.) through which they may be overruled or through which they may be directed. Hence this concept emphasizes, as does that of organization specialization, the factors of access and of relationships among forums of policy making.

Interaction

The tendencies toward concentration in institutional specialization and strategic location are made tolerable under democratic morality only if many countervailing factors distributing influence are present. One of these is a third institutional feature, described in the concept of *interaction*. The concept is that policy results from *the interaction of actors occupying strategic positions,* rather than from the behavior of a single person.

Within a single organization, decisions made through interaction are often called *institutional* (or group) decisions. They are decisions of an organization rather than of a person and result from the complementary contribution of men with different roles—e.g. of giving legal, economic, engineering, or management counsel. A clearance sheet may show the names of some of the actors, whose names in turn reflect the interaction of other persons at their levels or divisions of the organization. The decision integrates the interactions among contributors from various strategic locations.

Institutional decisions result from, and indeed are necessitated by, technicality and complexity of the problems on which decision is made. Technical information not available to a single person, or even usually to a single type of professional, is required for rational judgment. Further, diverse and interweaving interests will be affected by the decision. Hence, the organization aggregates and co-ordinates the competencies that it contains. Kenneth Galbraith has called all those who participate in group decision making, and the organizations formed by their participation, the "technostructure." [3] This technostructure may reflect a wide distribution of influences on decision making among many strategic centers in the organization.

Interactions are also *interinstitutional*. There is additional participation and a decision integrates the roles of men in strategic positions in different, perhaps many, organizations. For example, wage changes in a company are not usually determined solely by those within the company, but by the interaction of company or industry representatives, union

3. John Kenneth Galbraith, *The New Industrial State* (Boston: Houghton Mifflin Company, 1967), p. 71.

representatives, and government mediators. A policy decision in government may be the result of interactions among the President, members of Congress, administrative officials, private-association representatives, and a variety of consultants. Some amount of autonomy accrues to every organization, but each will be constantly limited by interactions with other organizations in the same functional complex. Moreover, there will be interaction among functional complexes (e.g. those in health and those in education, and those in research and development in armed services-industry) and between all the functional complexes and the top strategic positions in the government (e.g. the President and the Bureau of the Budget). The results are that forums of decision affecting varied interests are complexes of many interacting centers in many organizations and that the access of interested groups is broadened through inputs within these forums from numerous centers reflecting different interests. Access of interest groups is broadened by forums of decision that are inter-institutional.

A proposition may be stated at this point: *the attainment of the democratic ideal in the world of administration depends much less on majority votes than on the inclusiveness of the representation of interests in the interaction process among decision makers.*

INDIVIDUALS WITHIN INSTITUTIONS

Policy, we have now seen, is made or at least finally determined by interaction among strategic positions within organizations. But since men occupy those strategic positions, it is necessary to look for what is regular in the behavior of men who are in positions that give them opportunities to influence policies.

Clinical studies have now given validity to common-knowledge assumptions that men in strategic positions are influenced in many ways. They may, first, be influenced by their own personality traits. Writers have distinguished, for example, between authoritarian and permissive personalities.[4] It should be noted, however, that the impact of personality variations on policy will be limited by institutional factors—by the absorption of the individual into institutional behavior and the limitations upon him in the interaction process. It will vary also among organizations. The authoritarian personality in a hierarchical position, for example, may have less opportunity to influence decisions on a college faculty or in a scientific research organization than in a military organization or one with routine operations. Leadership—that is, the effective concentration of influence over the interaction process—may be more dependent upon personal adaptation to institutional factors than on inherent personality traits.

Men in strategic positions will also be influenced by the attitudes and standards of conduct prevailing in the society of which they are a part. Society's expectations of its policy makers have been aptly termed "rules of the game" by David Truman.[5] These rules may relate to the personal conduct of the policy maker and may vary according to position occupied: on matters of personal probity, for example, they may be tight for the administrative official, looser for the businessman dealing with him, and still looser for the relations between businessmen and politicians. The rules may also relate to expectations in social policy. The policy maker will be influenced by societal attitudes toward such varied things as budget balancing, the freedom of a man to use his

4. A considerable quantity of research and publication followed publication of T. W. Adorno, et al., *The Authoritarian Personality* (New York: Harper and Brothers, 1950). Robert Presthus, *The Organizational Society: An Analysis and a Theory* (New York: Random House, 1965), Chapters 6, 7, and 8, distinguished and discussed at length upward-mobiles, indifferents, and ambivalents in organizations.

5. David B. Truman, *The Governmental Process: Political Interests and Public Opinion* (New York: Alfred A. Knopf, 1951), particularly pages 159, 348–49, 441, 511–16.

property, the obligation of a man to support his family, the way a policeman should treat a private citizen, and the way a supervisor should treat an employee. Such attitudes will have a strong effect on whether men in strategic positions contribute by their efforts to policies that accord with democratic morality.

Official Role

I isolate for discussion three concepts that are especially relevant to individual behavior in organizations. The first relates to the ways men will behave because of their official positions. The concept is that of official role, which may be defined as the actual behavior of men because of the positions they occupy. Official roles are patterns of behavior induced by specialized positions, or by the rules and conventions of society for persons occupying positions.[6] This is a behavioral description based on what men *do* because of their position rather than on what is prescribed for them in formal rules.[7] But "official role" is also an institutional concept, for official roles are determined by organizational position. Behavior is in part anticipatable because it is determined by position. The term "role" can be used to refer to the total behavior of an individual. We are distinguishing here that part of role or behavior that is induced by position.

6. Charles E. Lindblom has said: *"The behavior of each participant (including each citizen) in the governmental process is greatly controlled by conventions about ends and means that have the effect of prescribing behavior conditionally or absolutely.*

"The conventions are explicit or implicit prescriptions that specify to some degree, though only very roughly, what goal values and side values can and cannot be sacrificed to the achievement of other values." *The Intelligence of Democracy: Decision Making Through Mutual Adjustment* (New York: The Free Press, 1965), p. 91.

7. The definition is an adaptation of that of Ralph Linton in *The Cultural Background of Personality* (New York, 1945), pp. 76–77, who defines it in terms of what we expect of a person in a particular *status*. In our definition, role is not function or duty, but *behavior* arising because of function or position.

The concept of role is illustrated in the clinical studies of Richard Fenno of the House Appropriations Committee. He finds there is a socialization process through which each member is integrated into the committee and led to behave in conformity with the committee's norms of conduct. The central norm is protection of the Treasury through the instrumental task of cutting budget estimates.[8] The official role, therefore, is budget trimming.

Official roles will normally have a foundation in formal allocation of duties. But they will take full form in the habits of the system in which they play a part. In the language of administration, they are created both formally and informally. The House Appropriations Committee is delegated the duty of scrutinizing appropriations. So is the Senate Appropriations Committee. Formally they have the same role. But Fenno finds that actually the role of the Senate Committee, in contrast to the budget-trimming role of the House committee, is to protect the agencies from harsh treatment and to safeguard constituency interests.[9]

The role structure of an organization usually is complex. Ralph Huitt's clinical study of a congressional committee showed a variety of official roles for senators. Their activities reflected roles as party leader, Administration spokesman, representative of a constituency interest, "errand boy" for particular constituents, representation of an industry's position, and so on.[10] In large administrative organizations, official roles are highly specialized. While in a legislative body they are assembled in the persons of legislators, in an administrative structure they are dispersed among numerous persons with specialized functions. Nevertheless, the closer action

8. Richard F. Fenno, Jr., "The House Appropriations Committee as a Political System: The Problem of Integration," *The American Political Science Review*, Vol. LVI (June 1962), pp. 310–24.
9. Richard F. Fenno, Jr., *The Power of the Purse: Appropriation Politics in Congress* (Boston: Little, Brown and Company, 1966), Chapters 3 and 10.
10. Ralph K. Huitt, "The Congressional Committee: A Case Study," *The American Political Science Review*, Vol. XLVIII (June 1954), pp. 340–65.

moves to the top of an organization, the more likelihood there is that the official roles will be multiple rather than single. What used to be known as homogeneity and heterogeneity of function can now be referred to as unity and variety in role. The total official role of a national department head will reflect the interests of the President and often also of the party, clienteles served by the department, staffs within the department, and his own view of the general interests and values of society. His total behavior, insofar as it is determined by his position, is the sum of these particular roles.

In a discussion of democracy several aspects of official roles are significant. First, interests are represented through official roles of legislators and administrators occupying individually strategic positions or assembled with others in agencies, committees, or other structures. Roles bring the representation of interests inside the government. They focus and magnify the representation of favored interests. By their continuity they also extend the representation of interests over time. Second, the policy maker's opportunity to influence representation of interests depends upon his ability to establish roles that provide continuing representation of those interests. For example, Congress sought to provide continuous representation of the interests in economy by establishing the Bureau of the Budget, and it has sought to provide for compromise between interests of consumers and interests of regulated companies by creating regulatory commissions. In such instances it creates agencies which in turn assemble roles of individuals within them.

Third, the ability of overhead political institutions to prescribe behavior is limited, not only by the complexity of interests pressing for continuous representation through established roles, but also by the complexities of organization itself. Conflicting interests do find representation: witness, for example, the conflicts between free trade interests, represented in the roles of men in the Department of State, and those of protectionists, represented in roles of those in the Departments of Commerce, Agriculture, and Labor. The complexities of organization, indeed, may even produce conflicting roles for a single actor. In a case study on the Children's Bureau, for example, it was shown that Miss Lenroot, the head of the Children's Bureau, faced a conflict between two roles arising out of her position—one as representative of the President, who desired reorganization of the bureau, the other as representative of clienteles, who did not want it.[11] Such a conflict of roles is common in administration.

It may be concluded that democratic morality may be achieved in an administered society through channeling political purpose into roles of individuals serving in specialized organizations. Sometimes political purpose can be embodied in rules that require no (or little) public administration and depend for their observance on private acceptance or enforcement. But normally purpose, organization, and rules set guides for roles of individuals. Through these rules, administration can serve the interests of policy makers, whether toward democratic or other values.

Personal Stakes

Behavior may be influenced in a second way, included in the concept of personal stakes.[12] This concept refers to the self-regarding element in administrative behavior. Behavior may be induced by a man's personal interest rather than by official position, or by the two in combination, and as a result the effort to represent interests of groups in society through official roles of actors in administration may be thwarted.

11. "The Transfer of the Children's Bureau," in Harold Stein, ed., *Public Administration and Policy Development: A Case Book* (New York: Harcourt, Brace and Co., 1952), pp. 15–29.
12. For a discussion of a political system in terms of "stakes and prizes" see Wallace S. Sayre and Herbert Kaufman, *Governing New York City: Politics in the Metropolis* (New York: Russell Sage Foundation, 1960), especially Chapter II.

Let me illustrate the mixture of personal stakes with official roles in organization behavior. A member of a board of directors of a corporation (i.e. an executive) votes on an increase in the compensation of executives. A department head in the government or a university president faces a problem with the knowledge that his decision on it may affect his own continuation in office. A congressman realizes that his vote on a matter of general interest may affect votes for him in the next election. Obviously, in all of these and in innumerable other situations personal stakes are mixed with official roles.

Men in positions of responsibility try generally to protect interests represented through official roles from contrary personal interests. One way is to keep personal stakes out of an organization through, for example, prohibition of various forms of conflicts of interest. But new personal stakes are created when men enter organizations, primarily those of survival and reward within the organization. These personal stakes are so important that their validity as claims on the organization are discussed separately in Chapter VII. Another way of protecting against personal stakes is to submerge them through institutional devices, as through strict definition of official duty, audit or inspection of performance, or requirement of collaboration of men who have different roles in the making of decisions. Another is to achieve identification of personal with organization purpose by socializing an individual into the organization. A policeman, fireman, or member of the armed forces is taught that his official role is more important than even his life; a forester is taught to think as a forester.[13] Duty, responsibility take the place of personal interest. The job absorbs the man.

Absorption may be so complete or conflict between organization purpose and personal interest may be so insignificant that a "zone of indifference" is created—an area in which

13. Herbert Kaufman, *The Forest Ranger: A Study in Administrative Behavior* (Baltimore: The Johns Hopkins Press, 1960), Chapter VI.

the individual accepts official duty without regard to personal benefit.[14]

Conflict between the two may, however, create tension for the individual and uncertainty as to which set of influences will prevail. *Profiles in Courage* tells us that some men will make the response required by official duty, but it records only the way exceptional men have sometimes acted in exceptional instances.[15]

For those whose life is politics—those who serve in representative positions—these approaches to safeguarding official roles are obviously inadequate. The Burkean ideal of duty and *Profiles in Courage* offer slim hope for the democrat. He has to hope that the system of representation will identify the personal stakes of representatives with the interests of all men in constituencies. This is what Neustadt has claimed for the presidency: ". . . what is good for the country is good for the President and *vice versa*." [16] I know of no similar claim for congressmen in general. The examples of a Southern congressman voting against minimum wages even though thousands of families in his constituency are underprivileged because of low wages, or against civil rights even though the rights of multitudes of men in his district are unprotected, are pertinent to the issue. Neustadt's assertion may be extravagant, for any man in public office may find conflicts between personal stakes and official responsibility. But the crucial question is: are the personal stakes of the representative determined by a democratic base of power? His dominant personal stake is re-election—or, in the case of a second-term President, it may be approval by election of his party's nominee. The democratic morality can be served only if he, concurrently with other representatives, is required to give attention to all the interests affected by decisions.

14. See Chester I. Barnard, *The Functions of the Executive* (Cambridge, Mass.: Harvard University Press, 1938), pp. 167–69.
15. John F. Kennedy, *Profiles in Courage* (New York: Harper & Row, 1955).
16. Richard E. Neustadt, *Presidential Power: The Politics of Leadership* (New York: John Wiley & Sons, Inc., 1960), p. 185.

Personal stakes may be identified with institutional stakes. For example, a public official may contemplate his own security and advancement through the permanence and expansion of the institution in which he serves. Those who serve in official roles are not usually unbiased personally on issues of agency survival and growth. This may, nevertheless, create no conflict with official role, indeed may lead to more vigorous effort in the official role.

Professionalization

The third kind of influence on behavior of men in organizations is included in the concept of professionalization.[17] "Professionalization" can be defined quite technically as entry, advancement, and tenure in organizations on the basis of specialized qualifications and performance. Or it can be defined more generally as the attitudes growing out of concentrations of training, interest, and function that affect the behavior of men within their positions.

Professionalization in a technical society is a necessary complement to official role. That is, official roles will not be effective in results unless the action taken is that of men who themselves possess, or are assisted by persons who possess, specialized qualifications and attitudes. For example, forest protection will not be effective unless it is executed by men who have learned how to perform specialized tasks such as fighting forest fires, and budget trimming or auditing will not be effective unless those responsible have acquired competences and attitudes appropriate to these tasks. At the same time professionalization can—like personal stakes—distort the behavior of those in official positions. It can bring about professional communities of interest and opinion different from interests that sought representation through official positions, and perspectives on policy that reflect the attitudes and

17. Relevant to this discussion is Frederick C. Mosher's *Democracy and the Public Service* (New York: Oxford University Press, 1968), particularly Chapter IV, "The Professional State."

interests of these professional communities. Bankers making monetary policy, doctors influencing health care policies, lawyers prescribing regulatory methods, and academicians determining research and teaching goals, all have policy orientations that reflect their professional experience and that may influence their behavior more than official prescription of duties.

THE DECISION MAKERS

This leads us into inquiry as to who the decision makers are in the administrative state. Do the people who occupy strategic positions in organizations form an oligarchy or set of oligarchies? Are we governed either by a professional elite or by a combination of elites? Or, in Galbraith's terminology, by a technostructure or set of technostructures?

We are met at the outset of this discussion by an argument that would make meaningless or relegate to secondary significance the questions just presented. It is the argument that decision makers within the administrative state, whoever they may be, are controlled by a "power elite" or "governing class." The enemy of democracy, from this perspective, is not the power of the occupants of the strategic positions in the administrative state but the concentration of power in an elite which integrates the administrative/political structure with a small leadership structure external to it. And the roles of administrators/politicians are significant only (or primarily) as an agency function for the elite. To the old view that administrators are agents is added the antidemocratic interpretation that they are agents of a small, identifiable portion of the society.

We must look briefly at this argument before further examining decision making through administrative structures. The power elite argument suggests "domination of the decisional process by *a single group or a few men*, limited rank-and-file access, little or no opposition, and a failure on the

part of the adult community to use   its   political resources
to influence important decisions." [18] There have been studies
that present considerable evidence of concentrated leadership in some local governments, although, as Robert Presthus
says, the data may show a continuum with varying degrees of
concentration and rank-and-file participation.[19] There have
been arguments also that there is a power elite that is able
"to realize its will" in the larger arena of national decision
making. There is "a top social stratum"—a "set of groups
whose members know one another," communicate with one
another, and are able by such means as contribution to campaign expenses and control of public executive positions to
dominate the political/administrative system. The chief elements of this elite, the argument runs, are corporate executives, the military leaders, and the political directorate
(chiefly the executives of departments), and these operate
coincidentally and with interchangeable occupants of positions. The masses are fragmented and powerless; and the
checks and balances within the political system through which
Congress, professional politicians, administrators (subordinate
to an executive overhead), and the middle classes exert influence can be effective only on middle- or lower-range issues.[20]

   In contrast to the argument that there exists a single elite
is Robert Dahl's conclusion, based upon a study of decisions

18. This definition of "elitism," is from Robert Presthus, *Men at the Top: A
Study in Community Power* (New York: Oxford University Press, 1964), p. 25.
Italics mine.
19. Ibid. Presthus provides in his book a useful summary of the empirical
findings in community power studies.
20. For further explanation see C. Wright Mills, *The Power Elite* (New York:
Oxford University Press, 1956), from which the quoted words and much of
the exposition in the text is taken; Floyd Hunter, *Top Leadership, U.S.A.*
(Chapel Hill, N.C.: The University of North Carolina Press, 1959); and William Domhoff, *Who Rules America* (Englewood Cliffs, N.J.: Prentice-Hall, Inc.,
1967). For an opposite view see Arnold M. Rose, *The Power Structure: Political Process in American Society* (New York: Oxford University Press, 1967),
and for a closely reasoned argument that the military is not a unified element
in a power elite see Morris Janowitz, *The Professional Soldier* (Glencoe, Ill.:
Free Press, 1960).

in New Haven, that different groups of persons control the making of policy in different program areas. While Dahl's data was limited to three areas (party nominations, urban redevelopment, and public education) in one city in one period of time, his conclusion is worthy of note:

> Probably the most striking characteristic of influence in New Haven is the extent to which it is *specialized;* that is, individuals who are influential in one sector of public activity tend not to be influential in another sector; and what is probably more significant, the social strata from which individuals in one sector tend to come are different from the social strata from which individuals in other sectors are drawn.[21]

In comparison with Dahl's data, which shows only a 6 per cent overlapping of leaders in issue areas, Presthus shows an overlap of 29 per cent in nine communities, including New Haven, that have been studied. The studies relate, however, to cities of less than 150,000, and Presthus concludes "that overlapping appears to be inversely associated with size." He says that "size is critical in determining the structure of community power. . . . It may well be that smaller communities just do not possess enough potential leaders to make possible a lively competition among organized groups." [22]

There is as yet no convincing body of empirical evidence sufficient to support the thesis that a single elite or group of elites either will have unity of will consistently, or power to prevail regularly, in the complex decision-making processes that characterize either the national government or the variety of functional complexes that transcend governmental divisions (national-state-city) or public-private divisions. One method of substantiating the thesis is to gather evidence on

---

21. Robert A. Dahl, *Who Governs? Democracy and Power in an American City* (New Haven: Yale University Press, 1961), p. 169. Corroboration of this conclusion is found in Roscoe C. Martin, Frank J. Munger, and others, *Decisions in Syracuse* (Bloomington: Indiana University Press, 1961).
22. Presthus, *Men at the Top*, pp. 420 and 45.

the membership of the top economic, military, and political leaders and to show their interlockings and interchangeability. The evidence of this type generally does not include tracing through particular decisions to show that the will of the elite prevailed. It is normally assumed that the top leaders prevail over lower levels in the executive structure and that Congress and other checks against executive power are ineffective; and emphasis is placed on the co-ordination of economic and political (or economic-military-political) power in some arenas of policy making without giving attention to others.

Another method of substantiating the thesis of elite control is to analyze the decision-making process as used for selected decisions. This method may penetrate more profoundly into the determinants of or influences on decisions, but the evidence obtained could not be sufficiently cumulative to warrant judgment on the total character of decision making in the variety of situations arising from the multiform program complexes. It is quite likely that there are great differences in the degree of elite control in the extensive panorama of decision-making situations. At this stage of our knowledge a continuum may be assumed with varying dedegrees of concentration of influence in different program complexes.

I am not able to present new empirical evidence on the class composition of the constituent elements in decision-making arenas or on the operation of the governmental system in the making of particular decisions. I can, however, suggest the value of another approach, at least as an initial framework for analysis, namely, the description of the interaction process in an administrative state imbedded in and operating as part of a political system. I shall not argue the degree of democracy in the political-administrative system; clearly we do not have the evidence for that and perhaps never will except for segments of the system. I shall argue that there are possibilities for a large degree of democracy

By way of introduction, I propose the thesis that *the system is more or less democratic in the degree to which the multiple strategic centers of interaction in decision making are, in their totality, responsive to the total variety of interests affected by the decisions.*

In later chapters (III to V) I shall analyze the great complexity of decision making in the national administrative-political system and demonstrate the extreme pluralism of the process. At this point let us concentrate on the internal decision makers and the factors in external influence upon them that may produce a reasonable attainment of the democratic morality.

Initially, it is suggested that the men who occupy the strategic positions in the national administrative system do not appear to constitute a single tight oligarchy. Some years ago James Burnham told us that we would be ruled by a managerial class—a view that may have been comforting to some who thought the public interest could be represented through an administrative class of generalist managers, but frightening to others who fear all types of oligarchy.[23] Victor Thompson, in turn, has told us that managers cannot rule over specialists.[24] Specialists, it can be added, are not a unified group in our society, and they are not likely to be in any industrialized society. We have some basis in this conflict of views for confidence in the dispersion of influences.

Don Price has recently divided decision makers into four estates—the scholarly (especially the scientific), the professional (lawyers, engineers, physicians, etc.), the administrative, and the political. Each of the four, he argued, has a different orientation and this creates a kind of check and balance system among decision makers.[25] This analysis is arresting,

23. James Burnham, *The Managerial Revolution: What Is Happening in the World* (New York: The John Day Company, 1941).
24. Victor A. Thompson, *Modern Organization* (New York: Alfred A. Knopf, 1961).
25. Don K. Price, *The Scientific Estate* (Cambridge, Mass.: Harvard University Press, 1965), pp. 132–36.

yet it seems to me we should inquire further: Are we governed by functional oligarchies, that is, oligarchies for each major program area?

We may answer, first, with this simple but quite significant proposition: *structural specialization along program lines* (discussed at the beginning of this chapter) *is, indeed, accompanied by specialization among decision makers.* Random illustrations in support of the proposition can be given:

1. Policy making positions in education are filled generally from the educational community—in colleges from those having Ph.D.s.
2. In the Forest Service almost every policy-making position is filled by persons who began work as foresters after being trained in forestry schools.
3. Scientists fill many of the key positions in NASA and other scientific agencies, and scientists have joined the military in a military-scientific complex in the military departments.
4. Regulatory functions are administered almost exclusively by lawyers through procedures that only lawyers are technically qualified to apply.
5. Tenure and seniority in committee posts have professionalized even the politicians in Congress.
6. Similar qualifications exist for service in organizations conducting identical or complementary programs in different jurisdictions, e.g. for health officers in national, state, and local governments.

This does not mean, however, that we are governed completely by independent functional oligarchies. There are many factors countering functional specialization. First, the professional communities are generally not closed, either in professional or in class terms. Additional types of professional competence besides that which is dominant will almost always be required in the organization. Entry, either of new professionals or of nonprofessionals, is often possible at any level of organization. This is restricted in Congress by seniority practices in committees and by the impossibility of rising to party leadership without experience in Congress. It is, however, facilitated in the executive branch by civil service rules and by the practice of placing political appointees in the top positions. Class exclusiveness of our officials is inhibited by many factors, such as entry into positions of authority by men of humble origin, the payment of middle-class salaries, the lack of differentiated symbols of status for public officials, and the insecurity of political occupancy.

Second, men are never completely professionalized. In our society their professional education follows extensive general education. Also, as members of society, professional men share the values that dominate or compete within it. Third, there is frequently lack of consensus among professionals. Price says scientists "have introduced into stodgy and responsible channels of bureaucracy the amiable disorder of a university faculty meeting"—thus suggesting the lack of consensus in two professional groups.[26] We know, of course, that economists reveal the same lack of unanimity about public policy. One effect of this diversity in views and judgments is that it gives opportunity to other types of professionals or to nonprofessionals to influence policy.

Fourth, there are, indeed, countervailing aggregations of specialists. For example, professionals in budgeting (process specialists) can from their strategic positions oppose program specialists. Specialists serving in overlapping and conflicting jurisdictions, even when sharing professional attitudes, are aligned against each other as official role prevails over profession. Moreover, policy cannot ordinarily be made without concurrent activity from men in two, three, or perhaps all of Price's four estates. The scientist requires the help of the bureaucrat and the strict professional (e.g. the lawyer), and all require the support of the politician. This is, it will be

26. Price, *The Scientific Estate*, p. 75.

apparent, only a restatement of Price's internal check and balance system.

These factors countering functional specialization are not, however, sufficient to provide democratic rather than oligarchic government. If the four estates operate within complexes, or subsystems, that are closed except for the entry of new personnel, then we will indeed be governed by functional oligarchies. There are strong tendencies in the administered society in this direction: the requirement of specialized knowledge for solution of problems, the institutional features which concentrate influence in strategic locations within separate program arenas, and the invisibility and complexity of the processes of decision within complex organizations. Even the politicians tend to be absorbed into arenas of specialized decision. To be democratic the processes of decision within functional complexes will have to be open to outside influence. Internal checks will have to be supplemented by external checks of power and opinion. The interaction process will have to be broadened beyond that comprised within the four estates.

That the interaction process is indeed broader will be apparent on further analysis. Price's four estates include the decision makers in government. Their strength is, of course, increased because they have memberships or associations outside government, but their impact on policy is achieved through their internal position. Price does not include three outside estates: the power brokers, the opinion makers, and the lay participants. These, too, get inside government, but their primary affiliations are outside. We need not be concerned about overlappings of the categories called estates, because the distinctions between these clarify roles in decision making.

The power brokers are the men who serve as intermediaries between the government and outside interests. This brokerage is part of the function of the men in government—particularly the politicians; but power brokers make up an estate outside the formal organization of government. The power brokers include primarily party workers and interest group representatives. In general the party workers are office-oriented and their primary function is to fill the elected offices of government. They take an interest also in policy and through joint and individual efforts can affect policy, but in our system the party function in policy making passes largely to the men the parties select as office holders—to the politicians inside government. The primary party function is to facilitate the electoral function, which will be discussed later.

The interest group (functional and class) representatives perform three functions in decision making. The first is to aggregate, compromise, and define the interests, and therefore the policy positions, of groups in the population. This is an important intermediary step in policy making. If performed successfully it will reveal to the ultimate policy makers the basic clusters of interests that exist. If performed openly it may reveal also the disunities within interest group communities. Let me illustrate from my studies of the Air Transport Association.[27] Its members are certificated commercial air carriers. These member companies have a common interest: a favorable regulatory climate that prevents entry of new companies, safeguards profits, provides safety, and in general promotes air transportation. They also have conflicting interests—for example, between trunklines and local service carriers, and between carriers in each category seeking expansion of their routes. The association will aggregate and define the common interest but leave to the individual companies the representation of their separate interests.

The second function of interest group representatives is to provide access to decisional forums for the common interests of the group. This means bringing to the attention of policy makers information on what the interests to be considered are,

27. See my study of the Air Transport Association in Emmette S. Redford, *The Regulatory Process: Illustrations from Civil Aeronautics* (Austin: The University of Texas Press, to be published in 1969), Chapter 6.

the number of units affected, the quantity of the interest, and the intensity of feeling on it. The third function is to participate in the bargaining through which an accommodation of interests is achieved. This may range from explicit bargaining (as in labor-management negotiations) through a middle range of bargaining (through advisory committees or representation on a government commission) to the bargaining implicit in the ability to cause a furor or prevent compliance with a decision.

The interest group communities, unlike the party organizations, are primarily interested in policy rather than office holding. Their effect is the inclusion of more organizations and more men in the policy-making arena. Their representatives are additional strategic centers through which influence is brought to bear on public policy. On its face the interest group community appears to broaden participation and to increase the representation of interests.

Whether it in fact broadens or narrows the representation of interests will be dependent upon the total forces operating in particular policy-making forums at a given time. In general, group organization tends to aggregate two types of interest which may exist separately or in fusion. One is the intensity interest—the interest that, while it may be dispersed among many people and not be a major factor in self-realization for most of them, may yet be held with sufficient intensity by some persons to make possible its aggregation by organizational effort. Men have wanted prohibition, cancer research, or parkland extension enough to lead them to join organizations for these purposes. The other is the high-quantity interest, normally the interest in economic gain. Low-intensity and low-quantity interests tend not to be represented. And there is unevenness in the representation of interests, even the high-quantity interests. Thus, for example, the interests of some workers, such as automobile workers, are much more effectively represented than those of other workers, such as department store personnel. When this unevenness exists, it may be reflected in a narrowing of the role of public officials to the extent that they reflect only the interests of the strongly organized.

There are two answers to this unevenness which accord with democratic morality. One is an open society in which all groups have opportunity for organization. This is not a complete answer, first because man cannot organize all of his interests, second because the right to organize is not always accompanied by opportunity. Opportunity may be limited by such factors as dispersion (e.g. in the case of agricultural workers), low status (migrant laborers), and lack of permanence of interest (as where there is mobility among trades). The other answer is that by virtue of other kinds of influence on policy making—voting, demonstrations, and so on—the weakly organized or unorganized interests may be represented in the roles of decision makers.

Another estate may be described as the opinion makers. It too is not entirely separate from the estates within government, but it extends beyond them. Here, as in the case of other factors, we find concentrations and dispersions of influence.

Usually the discussion of opinion making centers around information given in the mass media. Whether the mass media provide the public with opportunity for informed, rational judgment is indeed an important issue of democracy. I want, however, to call attention to certain other aspects of decision making. The first is the influence of professional opinion, developed by exchange of ideas within professional communities. In law reviews, scientific journals, and journals of professional discussion in such areas as education and welfare; in professional conferences; and in books and monographs ideas are exchanged within the professional communities. I have used the plural term, "communities," because these exchanges reflect the specializations referred to earlier. There is no single establishment of ideas, as there is none of power. Moreover, the functional specialists among the opinion makers include men serving in organizations independent of government control, and this expands the protections against functional oligarchy beyond those operating within official organizations.

Second, important to policy making are the breakthroughs of lead ideas or impulses from professional or other sources. Let me illustrate by examples of past breakthroughs:

> Churchill's speech at Fulton, Missouri, Secretary Marshall's speech at Harvard, and George F. Kennan's article in *Foreign Affairs*, initiated American policy stances with respect to the Cold War, foreign aid, and containment, respectively.[28]

> John Maynard Keynes's books provided intellectual support for American fiscal policy.

> Charles Hitch's activity in the Department of Defense inaugurated PPBS.

> Ralph Nader's *Unsafe at Any Speed* led to legislation on safety installations on automobiles.[29]

> Martin Luther King's leadership of the civil rights movement supported nonviolent protest and marches to bring attention to reform goals.

Third, the bridges between opinion makers and politicians are important. Politicians in this age of specialization cannot move far with policy positions that have no support in the communities of knowledge—they are blocked if their solutions are not technically feasible, and probably also if they affront the entrenched functional specialists. On the other hand, the knowledge communities are estopped from ruling society by the necessity of obtaining support from the politicians.

28. See George F. Kennan, "The Sources of Soviet Conduct," *Foreign Affairs*, Vol. XXV (July 1947), pp. 556–83.
29. *Unsafe at Any Speed: The Designed-In Dangers of the American Automobile* (New York: Grossman, 1965).

Fourth, the opinion makers must find a response in the public. They will find there a complex of many objective interests and subjective attitudes, and also some elements of consensus. On nearly every issue high-quantity interests will be aroused, and they will resort to their specialized channels of access; on some issues the diffused interests of the public will be affected sufficiently to engage response from large numbers of people. The opinion maker on matters of public policy is ultimately face to face with the public.

We must note, also, lay entry into strategic positions. Lay participation is sometimes difficult to distinguish from professional or organizational affiliation. Nevertheless, examples readily verify its existence. School board membership normally appeals to lay persons rather than professionals in politics. Advisory or policy-making boards are common in such areas as hospital, library, and parks administration. Lay persons may even be brought into national councils: thus over three-fourths of the members of the National Commission on the Selective Service, appointed by the President in 1966, had had no kind of experience that could be called professional with respect to selective service policy. Strictly lay participation is, nevertheless, more exceptional than usual in modern specialized forums of policy making.

THE EIGHTH ESTATE: THE NONLEADERS

Our analysis has revealed the leadership structure of the administered society as complex, diversified, and distributed among many strategic centers of influence. Many of us are participants—regularly or occasionally, casually or purposefully, intimately or remotely—in the broadly inclusive interaction process among strategic centers of influence interacting in some areas of public policy.

This by itself does not mean that the administrative state is democratic. Many of us will be weak participants in the arenas of our participation, and all of us will be inactive in many other arenas in which our interests are affected. We are all part of an eighth estate—the nonleaders who are subject to the total structure of the administered society but who are not regularly active in most policy-making forums affecting their interests.

The first characteristic of the great body of men subject to the administrative state is that they are dormant regarding most of the decisions being made with respect to them. Their participation cannot in any manner equal their subjection. Subjection comes from too many directions for man's span of attention, much less his active participation, to extend to all that affects him. Any effort of the subject to participate in all that affects him would engulf him in confusion, dissipate his activity, and destroy the unity of his personality. Democracy in the sense of man's participation in all that affects him is impossible in the administered society.

The democrat must hope nevertheless that nonleaders can participate meaningfully at two levels at which policy is made: *first, that nonleaders generally (all or most) will have opportunity to share in influence on the men in the political superstructure who make the key political decisions on rules for society and roles for men occupying strategic positions in the arenas of functional specialization; and second, that representative portions of the population will have opportunities to participate selectively in influences on leaders occupying the strategic positions in the various arenas of program specialization in which decisions are made.*

The means of selective participation in the open society are diverse and numerous. The participation may be aggressively active, moderately active, or relatively silent but potentially active. In the administrative structures of the state, leaders in strategic positions must take account of the rank and file within their organizations. Administrators, scholars, professionals, and politicians must react to the activities and attitudes of their lesser colleagues within and outside the structures within which they work. The party leaders are influential only to the extent that they are able to be effective brokers of the interests of their followers. The interest group representatives can survive only if they represent the interests of nonleaders sufficiently to prevent their revolt and their formation and use of other channels of representation. The opinion makers can be effective only if they gain favorable response from a wider circle of people who think about specialized problems. Every group of leaders dealing with important issues is conscious of tension in his own position, arising only in part from the interaction with other leaders, but also from the activity and latent interests of the rank and file affected by their specialized activity.

For influence on the key decision makers in the political superstructure the ballot is the regular and recurring instrument of the nonleaders. A free and equal ballot for all is still the basic instrument of democratic government. The ballot has two overriding consequences: *it forces the politician to try to keep government under his control; and it forces him not only to listen to his constituents but to search for policies that promote their interests.* The former creates hope for a measure of political supremacy over the administered society; the latter, although it may degenerate into the lowest form of demagoguery, is nevertheless the essence of democratic leadership.

The ballot may speak strongly on some issues, only faintly on others; on many it speaks not at all. The skilled politician will know the "zones of indifference" in the electorate—the issues it is content for the moment to leave to the organization complexes—and will be conscious of the resentments and demands of his constituents. He may be aided in the future toward measurement of discontents and anticipations by the further scientization and wider use of poll taking.

Nonparticipation in elections and silence between elections have been weaknesses in the structure of public participation in the past. We may be in a period of change with respect to both. Voting rights have been extended and new groups of voters are coming to the polls. Greater activation of public expression between elections is evident in movements of public protest and demand. Through meetings, petitions and proclamations, and mass demonstrations, participation is being activated among many who heretofore were quiescent subjects of the administered society. The resorts to rioting are frightening, and the legitimacy of methods which border on or are in fact civil disobedience raise hard issues of democratic theory; but the energizing of participation among those who have been silent subjects—mostly youth and minority races—can only be welcomed by the believer in democratic morality.

The ultimate weapons of public expression are revolution and civil disobedience. The former cannot change the fundamental features of an administered society, and it is not likely to create any new instruments of continuing democratic control. The latter has been a recurring part of public expression —from the Boston Tea Party and the Whiskey Rebellion, through the resistance to fugitive slave laws, through violation of Prohibition, to draft-card burning. It cannot be welcomed by the democrat as a normal means of expression; on the other hand, he will be reminded by past events that the restrictions of the administered society must win general acceptance in the society. These weapons are evidence that those who govern must be cognizant of the nonparticipating public, that majorities are not enough on matters that touch deeply the vital interests of people—that in an open society the consensus for policy must be broad and deep.

SUMMARY

In the administrative state policies are made by the *interaction of men occupying strategic positions in specialized institutions.* Men's actions in these positions are the result of many factors, including especially their *official roles, personal stakes,* and *professional orientations.* These decision makers in government do not constitute a monolith, and while there are tendencies toward concentration of decision making in functional oligarchies there are many factors that moderate this concentration. Power is dispersed among many organization centers and among different categories of men, classified by Price into four estates—scholars, professionals in a strict sense, administrators, and politicians. The interaction process leading to decisions includes, in addition, three other groups which can also be called estates, namely, the power brokers outside government, the opinion makers, and the strictly lay participants in policy-making centers. Outside all these groups of participants is the eighth estate—all of us who as non-leaders are subjects of the administered society but are not regular participants in most arenas of decision making. Though normally dormant with respect to most arenas of policy, the nonleaders can exert influence through their access to leaders in areas of functional specialization, and through the ballot, demonstrations, and other means to key policy makers with general jurisdiction.

Policy is, in sum, made by interaction among minorities of men in strategic positions. The process can be called democratic only if the interaction process is broadly inclusive at two levels of decision making: first, at the level of political superstructure, where basic decisions on rules for society and roles for actors in the administrative state are made, and second, at the level of program specialization to which much of the decision making of the administrative state has been committed. The interaction process must include the participation of several types of leaders who through the diversities reflected in their participation and the influence of nonleaders upon them give representation to the manifold common and varied interests within the society.

III

Interaction in the

National Administrative System

It is now time to focus discussion on the central mechanism of the administrative state—the political-administrative system in Washington. It will be clear from the preceding chapter that the public administrative institutions of the administrative state can be interpreted and evaluated in their broadest and most significant dimensions only as they are considered as aspects of the total political system. In three chapters I shall sketch the administrative system in our national government and discuss three levels of politics operating through that system. I shall be interested in locating the strategic centers of influence, describing the effects of their interaction, and showing the implications for democratic morality.

THE TRADITIONAL MODEL OF
DEMOCRATIC ADMINISTRATION

Traditional literature on administration and politics gave us a model of how the administrative state ought to operate—a model that acquired orthodoxy in both administrative and democratic theory. It was a simple model of overhead democracy. It asserted that democratic control should run through a single line from the representatives of the people to all those who exercised power in the name of the government. The line ran from the people to their representatives in the Presidency and the Congress, and from there to the President as chief executive, then to departments, then to bureaus, then to lesser units, and so on to the fingertips of administration. Exceptions to the single line were acceptable only for the judiciary, and perhaps also for certain quasi-judicial and quasi-legislative functions and the auditing function.

The model was underpinned by four concepts. One was integration—the idea that units of administration should be linked in a single line of responsibility leading upward to the chief executive. The second was hierarchy—the idea that responsibility should be enforced through power exercised through successive levels of organization, each controlling the level immediately below it. The third was legality—that rules made at top levels in the hierarchy should guide the action of men at all subordinate levels. The fourth was political supremacy—that administration should be subordinate to political direction and supervision exercised through law and hierarchical oversight.

Few, if any, would deny that the overhead route is an essential means of implementing democratic morality in the administered society. Purpose—reflecting interests of clienteles to be served—must be defined somewhere and then embodied in practice. Representatives of the people are the primary channel for statement and enforcement of purpose. We have seen that one means of representing people is through definition of the roles to be played by men in administrative structures. I believe also that no one will deny that there is some measure of validity in all of the concepts that underpin the traditional model.

Nevertheless the traditional model is simplistic. It does not adequately define administration as it operates in Washington or as it may be expected to operate in spite of any reform efforts. Consideration of the possibilities for realization of democratic government must take account of more intricate administrative relationships than those described in the traditional model.

The web of interrelationships that creates the official universe of political-administrative activity in Washington is presented on Chart II. The chart, like charts generally, links positions. This is based on the assumption that position is important—either because behavior is institutionalized as official role or because position creates opportunity for non-official behavior to be influential in organizational activity. The chart, again like charts generally, assumes that what happens in complex structures is the result mainly of institutional interaction, that is, of the channeling of individual behavior through official positions. It is possible, of course, to assume purely private relationships among men holding official positions, as when brothers serving in Congress and as head of an administrative department talk at breakfast about the responsibilities of one of them; but this is quite exceptional in the relations of men each holding official position—their interaction usually reflects instead their roles in their separate positions. It is this that makes it possible for us to talk about system and order in administrative relationships.

The interrelationships that form the interaction system can be described by five colors, four of which appear on the chart. Each describes part of the total system. The lines on the chart represent two-way channels of interaction. In traditional organization theory it is said that authority descends and responsibility ascends on the lines; but in practice, as we shall see, this is gross simplification.

The blue-line system describes the pattern of the administrative line of direction, supervision, and responsibility as we have known it in traditional literature. It begins with

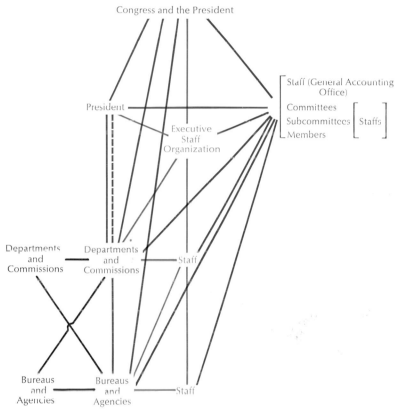

Chart II The Web of Political-Administrative Activity in Washington

the law-making-appropriating-supervisory power possessed jointly by the President and the houses of Congress. It shows, however, initiation at other points within the line, as when the President or a department head creates organization, allots functions, or makes policy.

The blue-line system is not a single line. The law-making power (Congress and the President) makes delegations to and specifications with respect to action by departments, commissions, or other agencies at that level. This legally circumvents the President as chief administrator, and the legal circumventions create practical limits on what he can do through his constitutional and political position. One need only mention the somewhat different position of the President with respect to regulatory commissions and to departments to bring to attention the potentialities of congressional short-circuiting of the Presidency.[1]

The short-circuiting is not limited, however, to the commissions. Congress regularly exercises a directive power over all parts of the government. It has, for example, legislated on the organization of the Department of Defense and on operations within it; it has even legislated on the way the Executive Office of the President shall be organized, as in legislation creating the Bureau of the Budget, Council of Economic Advisers, and National Security Council.

The Constitution divided the function of direction of administration, giving to Congress, on the one hand, the power to choose "necessary and proper" means of carrying out policy and to the President, on the other, the general powers to appoint officials and "to take care that the laws be faithfully executed," together with such specific powers as those contained in the commander-in-chief clause. The struggle of the

1. The President's position is shown in Emmette S. Redford, "The President and the Regulatory Commissions," *Texas Law Review*, Vol. XLIV (December 1965), pp. 288–321, and in David M. Welborn, "Presidents, Regulatory Commissions and Regulatory Policy," *Journal of Public Law*, Vol. XV (1966), pp. 3–29.

President and Congress for position, and the separate influences operating on each, have assured that the constitutional dualism would develop into a shared directorship of administration between the legislative and the executive power.

The chart shows parallel lines between the Presidency and department and commission heads (as might have been done elsewhere on the chart) to indicate that the relationship may be strong and continuous (unbroken line) or attenuated and intermittent (dotted line). The strength of the line will be the result, however, of other factors as well as the legal one. Thus the President's attention may be given continuously to the Departments of Defense and State, for example; but the limitations on his span of attention and interest, and the potential losses of his influence through intervention, may limit his attention to the Antitrust Division of the Department of Justice, the Communications Commission, or the Forest Service in the Department of Agriculture. Politics and events, as well as the varying visibility and insistence of the programs, strengthen or attenuate the lines of presidential influence, and conversely the opportunities of those at the level below him to interact with him. A former Secretary of State has said that he saw the President "almost every day, and rarely less than four times a week," [2] but some department heads struggle to get an occasional word with him at the end of Cabinet meetings. There is nothing more pathetic in administration than the effort of a subordinate to draw support from a line of contact that is formally open to him but is nevertheless not available.

The lines run also from Congress to bureaus or agencies within departments. President Truman, following recommendations of the first Hoover Commission, tried through reorganization proposals to have delegations to bureaus transferred to departments. He had much but not complete suc-

2. Dean Acheson, "The President and the Secretary of State," in Don K. Price, ed., *The Secretary of State* (Englewood Cliffs, N.J.: Prentice-Hall, Inc., 1960), Chapter 2, p. 45.

cess. Congress, for example, refused to allow the Secretary of the Treasury more than "general direction" over the Comptroller of the Currency. More important, however, than the direct vesting of duties in bureaus are the numerous congressional expectations with respect to the way they shall operate. For example, if the Secretary of Agriculture were to contemplate uniting all farmer-oriented programs into one line of control from Washington to the local offices he would find among other things that Congress has prohibited regional offices for the Farmers Home Administration, has prescribed a system of state co-operation for the Soil Conservation Service, and is committed to a system of farmer committees for administration of the functions of the Agricultural Stabilization and Conservation Service. He would probably conclude that it was better to leave the conservation functions which all three agencies have, and other related functions as well, under separate administration than to seek amendment of the several pieces of legislation related to each.

The green-line system describes the relationships of specialized staffs operating at successive levels in the administrative hierarchy. (Although I shall use the word "staff" or the term "specialized staffs," I wish to deny any assumption of clean separation of so-called "line" and "staff" functions.[3]) The second line of relationships, described as the green-line system, can exist between specialized personnel (e.g. scientists) operating at two levels who are deeply involved in the primary purposes of the hierarchical structure as well as between specialists who are performing so-called auxiliary (or facilitative) functions, such as budgeting, personnel, legal, or public relations duties. Any of these latter functions can, of course, be as deeply involved in primary or substantive planning and execution as any other activity.

The concept reflected by the green-line structure can be set

3. For a comprehensive analysis of line and staff relationships, see Robert T. Golembiewski, *Organizing Men and Power: Patterns of Behavior and Line-Staff Models* (Chicago: Rand McNally & Company, 1967).

forth in four propositions. First, certain specialized functions or activities get separately structured and professionalized at successive levels of organization. Second, this gives rise to additional lines of communication downward and upward. Lines of contact develop between the Civil Service Commission and the personnel officers of departments, and between the personnel officers of departments and those of bureaus; between budget offices at successive levels; and between attorneys at these levels. Third, these lines can be conveyor belts for distinct purposes complementing or conflicting with those in other channels of contact. For example, the objective of tight accounting on the uses of government funds and that of assuring equal pay for similar work are enforced through the activity of layers of accounting and personnel officials, respectively. The purpose of preventing racial discrimination in employment, although it will need the support of so-called line officials, will be achieved mainly through the continuous activity of personnel officers within departments carrying out detailed prescriptions of the Civil Service Commission.

Finally, these lines of contact between specialists at successive levels may be sufficiently strong to create a dualism in administrative supervision and responsibility. Many officials of government have learned that there is a dualism in the position of specialized staffs. I recall my own dismay, as a neophyte in administration, upon learning that the budget officer of the Rationing Department of the Office of Price Administration, who reported to me, had lunch daily with the budget officers at higher levels (to which he aspired to rise) and had acquired a budget-trimming attitude not in accord with the budget-raising needs his immediate superior thought existed. I recall too that, when all the division directors in a department of the agency threatened to resign unless lawyers attached to their divisions were told to serve only as their obedient counsel, the head of the agency responded that he intended that those lawyers serve as a restraint against the dangers resulting from their chiefs' business orientations.

The green-line system, you will note, shows contacts both between staff specialists and their "line" supervisors and among the specialists themselves.

The red-line system describes the relationships between positions within Congress and those within the executive branch. Congress, in addition to expression through votes of the houses, acts through committees, subcommittees, staffs of these and of the Congress (particularly the General Accounting Office), and through individual members representing constituents and holding strategic positions within the congressional organization. Each of these numerous centers within Congress is in interaction with numerous centers within the executive structure.

The interaction system between parts of Congress and parts of the executive results from two factors. In part it grows out of the representative system which establishes 535 centers of influence on administration and legislation. Contacts between these and administrative centers are made selectively, with initiatives emanating from both sides. Many of these are intermittent, but some of them harden into continuous lines of communication as similarities in interest develop. Every congressman has points of interest in administrative operations and every agency finds supporters in the congressional membership. In addition, these relationships feed on congressional specialization paralleling the specialization within the executive branch. These specializations create official roles within Congress vis-à-vis administration, and also new personal stakes of members in the maintenance of positions through which influence can be exerted on administration. Thus hard lines of contact and mutual interaction develop between congressional and administrative centers having related roles.

The interaction system is exceedingly complex. The most numerous contacts are between those in the agencies with program and budget roles and those in the related program and appropriations committees in Congress. But there are

also crosscutting lines of contact. Thus the General Accounting Office, the Government Operations committees, and the
appropriations committees, were in 1967 in contact with the
accounting officials of departments with respect to revision
of their accounting systems, and the complexity of the web
of relationships was increased by the lack of concordance in
viewpoint among the several congressional positions. The
red-line system, it will be noted, makes direct contact both
with the blue-line and the green-line systems.

The number of centers in Congress from which influence
can be exerted upon administration has increased as congressional specialization and staff have increased. Today specialization is mainly reflected in twenty standing committees in
the House, sixteen in the Senate, eleven joint committees of
the two houses, numerous subcommittees, and a number of
special committees. Moreover, the intrusiveness of Congress
is apparently increasing, and with it the amount of time given
within administration to congressional contacts. The intrusiveness referred to is that exercised through the parts of
Congress (the red-line system) rather than through the joint
direction of administration by the President and Congress
(the blue-line system), though the latter also exists. Committees direct administration on ways policies embodied in law
shall be administered. Sometimes the committees are able to
get authorization for their direction in legislation or appropriation riders—i.e. through the blue-line system. Presidents
occasionally try to buck this trend. For example, when Congress has sought to provide that administrative action shall
not be taken unless it is approved by committees of the Senate
and the House of Representatives, Presidents have on occa-
sions either vetoed the bills or after signing them refused to
execute the statutory provisions.[4]

4. See, for examples and for discussion of the constitutional issue—including
presentations pro and con by respected authorities—*Congressional Record,*
Vol. CXIII, pp. 14671–81 (October 11, 1967); and see also the veto message
of President Johnson on the Military Authorization Act of 1965 (August 21,
1965), *Congressional Record,* Vol. CXI, p. 21244.

More often this direction of administration is informal: a suggestion that action be taken or money be used in certain ways, a request for a report on what has been done when appropriation is considered, a statement that the committee expects policies to be changed or money used in the ways its members desire.

Congressmen occupying strategic positions—e.g. committee or subcommittee chairmanships—may be able to damage or benefit a bureau more than the departmental overhead to which it reports. Moreover, the seniority system in committees and the tenure of top bureau officials make both sides conscious of the fact that they may be doing business with each other for a long time, whereas the departmental political hierarchy may deal with neither for very long. The official roles and the personal stakes on each side of the congressional-administrative relationships are understood by people who work regularly together to produce accommodations between the two sets of positions. As a result of these factors, bureau chiefs may be more sensitive to congressional than to departmental direction. The red-line system may comprise firmer relations than the blue-line system.

Because of the potentialities for congressional control through the red-line system, and the expansion of presidential planning of the legislative program, Samuel Huntington has suggested that the most significant role for Congress in the future lies in administrative supervision rather than legislation.[5] Under this reasoning the coexistence of the red-line and the blue-line systems would be accepted as legitimate and desirable.

A fourth system, the brown-line system, represents lateral relationships between units of organization having responsibilities for different programs or parts of programs. The system is indicated but not elaborated on the chart. To be complete the chart would have to show lines for bureau-to

5. Samuel P. Huntington, "Congressional Responses to the Twentieth Century," in David B. Truman, ed., *The Congress and America's Future* (Englewood Cliffs, N.J.: Prentice-Hall, Inc., 1965), pp. 5–31.

bureau relations within departments, department-to-department and bureau-to-bureau relations across departments, professional-to-professional relations laterally between organizations, and committee-to-committee relations within Congress as jurisdictions overlapped.

Lateral relations are means of achieving co-ordination or accommodation without resort to the blue-line system. They may be accompanied by some measure of primacy to one of the collaborators, e.g. as when the Office of Economic Opportunity is delegated primary responsibility for co-ordinating antipoverty programs in various agencies, or the Department of Agriculture is given a similar responsibility with respect to rural development. Lateral relationships creating conflicts are, on the other hand, the most common cause of activity at higher levels in the blue-line system.

The brown-line system grows and increases in intimacy as government programs become more interrelated. The State and Defense departments collaborate through many interdepartmental committees and each must collaborate with numerous other departments or agencies. Welfare agencies must co-operate with each other and with educational, labor, and other agencies. It is doubtful whether it is now possible to delegate the whole of any major function of government to a single agency. Hence the brown-line system grows and the business moving along the blue lines increases.

CONCLUSIONS

What conclusions may be drawn from the discussion of this analytic model of patterns of relationship? I begin with three general conclusions. First, administrative relations are multi-directional: they flow upward and downward and laterally in varied channels. The model gives the lie to the monistic theory of public administration—the theory that authority moves down a single line. Second, there is co-direction of administration through executive and congressional channels. Neustadt's description of American government as "separated institutions sharing powers" applies clearly to the administrative function.[6] The model also gives the lie to the doctrine of separation of powers in its classic form, which assumes separated institutions concerned with separated types of power. In the American polity, administration is not a function solely of the executive branch; it is a continuing function of both the legislative and executive branches, exercised through parallel hierarchies in the two branches interacting with each other. Third, the model emphasizes differences in public and private administration, first in the greater complexity in public administration of the brown-line and green-line relationships, but much more in the coexistence of the red-line system. Democracy in public administration is greatly affected by this red-line system.

Further comment about the system may be helpful for our later discussion. Every position, whether in Congress or in the executive branch, has its own official role or sets of roles and every actor has his own stakes. Second, every line is a two-way channel of communication. Third, every line of communication is a potential channel of influence for interests represented in both the official roles and the personal stakes of actors.

Finally, a fifth element must be added to the model to make it complete. The first four elements describe only an internal system. But as noted in the last chapter, influences on policy in the administrative state extend beyond the interactions among public officials. There are influences from the outside interacting with those inside, which by choice of another color I will call the gray-line system. A graphical presentation would show an enormously complex system. It would include all the lines of influence from party officials, interest organizations, opinion makers, and the unorganized public. Some might suppose that the color gray gives oppor-

6. Richard E. Neustadt, *Presidential Power: The Politics of Leadership* (New York: John Wiley & Sons, Inc., 1960), p. 33.

tunity to emphasize the blending in external influences of the pure white of persuasion with the black magic of monetary bargaining, but this line of thought would have justified the choice of gray for other systems as well. The important conclusion for us here is that there is external politics which beams upon the internal politics that will produce policy in the administered society. We turn in the next two chapters to the three levels of politics, mixing internal and external influences, which affect the realization of democratic morality.

IV

Micropolitics and Subsystem Politics

IN THE COMPLEX of internal and external politics, concentrating influence and distributing it among centers of interaction, we can identify three kinds or levels of politics, differentiated by the scope of participation or involvement normally characteristic of each. I have elsewhere called these micropolitics, subsystem (or intermediary) politics, and macropolitics.[1] Micropolitics is that in which individuals, companies, and communities seek benefits from the larger polity for themselves. Subsystem or intermediary politics is the politics of function, involving the interrelations of bureaus and other administrative operating agencies, the counterpart congressional committee structure, and the interest organizations, trade press, and lobbyists concerned with a particular area of program specialization. Macropolitics is produced when the community at large and the leaders of the government as a whole are brought into the discussion and determination of policy. In this chapter I discuss the problems of reflecting democratic morality in micro- and subsystem politics.

MICROPOLITICS AND DEMOCRATIC MORALITY

An individual seeks a job in a public position, the waiving of a traffic violation, a change in his tax assessment, or some

1. In my *American Government and the Economy* (New York: The Macmillan Company, 1965), especially pp. 58ff.

other benefit related to his welfare. A company seeks a contract, waiver of an antitrust suit, the favorable location of a government improvement, a television license, or some other benefit. A community seeks to obtain from the national government funds for public housing, a grant for an airport, or a decision to locate a research laboratory or field office within its borders. What characterizes these things, first of all, is the differentiated, high-quantity interest of one or a few in a society of numerous persons, firms, or communities. In such situations microdecisions—that is, decisions applicable to one or a few—will have to be made. A second characteristic is the narrow involvement in the decisional process. It does not engage the broad participation in society that marks macropolitics, nor does it usually engage the response of effective countervailing interests. These decisions are "distributive," or "patronage," and "in the short run . . . can be made without regard to limited resources." Hence they can be made in situations which "approximate what Schattschneider called 'mutual non-interference' "—a mutuality where each seeks indulgences for himself and does not oppose those of others.[2]

There is nothing in democratic morality that denies the legitimacy of consideration of differentiated, high-quantity interests, whether of a group, of a community, or of an individual who regards satisfaction of these interests as important to his personal realization. On the other hand, even minimal regard for the equalitarian tenet of democratic morality requires that decisions regarding such interests be made with consideration of their effects on related or competing interests, and on the diffused interests of the community as a whole. In this kind of situation, democratic morality calls

2. The quotations are at pages 690 and 693 of the highly perceptive article of Theodore J. Lowi titled "American Business, Public Policy, Case-Studies, and Political Theory" and appearing in *World Politics*, Vol. XVI (July 1964), pp. 673–715. Lowi distinguishes between three kinds of policy "arenas": "distributive," "regulatory," and "redistributive." The distributive category parallels my micropolitics category.

for protective arrangements that will prevent eclipse of the equalitarian principle by favoritism to selected portions of the society. It calls for defense against the micropolitics that can create such favoritism. Micropolitics can debase politics and administration and consequently the moral tone of a community. An aristocracy may accept this debasement as part of its system of differential awards to favored groups, but favoritism obtained by special influence on microdecisions cannot be reconciled with the equalitarian ideal in democratic morality.

The basic response of democratic morality to micropolitics is to eliminate or subordinate it by programming for objective, impersonal administrative decision. The arguments for this answer are ethical; they are also political and administrative. The ethical standard that is consonant with democratic morality is equal treatment for all in like circumstances. This principle, inherent in the rule of law, is basic to democratic government. The political argument is that politics is debased when it becomes an instrument for differential advantage to some and like claims of others are not honored. The administrative argument is that many of the claims are —or, if honored, would be—recurrent, and that programming of repetitive claims in institutions is, like habit in individual behavior, a means of conserving time and energy. On the other hand, elimination of micropolitics may in many cases require complex and expensive process.

How can microdecisions—those that are potential subjects of micropolitics—be programmed? By three means, used separately or concurrently. The first is to create a rule or standard that will govern in most or all microdecisions of a type. The rule may be absolute, e.g. that every person who receives a traffic ticket for running a red light must pay $5.00 unless he goes to court and produces countervailing evidence that he did not move on the red signal. The rule may be a standard or set of standards which by itself produces only a first step toward decision, as in the case of multiple standards

that exist for determining which of several persons will get a
television license.[3] Policy may aim toward progressive extension and refinement of standards. Even exceptions may become rules of future practice. A college dean once told me
that every exception to rule made by him was immediately
distributed to his staff as a new standard to govern all like
situations arising in the future. A rule filed in the Federal
Register during World War II stated that the Administrator
or Assistant Administrator of Rationing could make an exception to any rule of eligibility for rations provided he filed
a finding that the exception could be extended to all persons
in like circumstances.

The second means of programming microdecisions is to
sink in administrative process the application of policy to
particular situations. This means, first, some kind of process
for getting the relevant and material facts on a record and,
second, internal processes to see that the record is not disre-
garded. Procedures may take the form of a judicialized process
in which hearings are held to build or test the record. In
this case there will be dangers of both underjudicialization
and overjudicialization with respect to the particular substantive action to be taken. More frequently it will take the
form of an administrative process, subject perhaps to an opportunity for a final judicialized appeal. An example is found
in Social Security administration, where an administrative
record of earnings, age, and other facts about an individual
determines who will get how much money and when; only
rarely is there substantive disagreement on facts or governing
rules of law such as produces the need for an opportunity for
appeal for re-examination through judicial processes.

A correct and adequate record is essential, whether it be a
policeman's report of a traffic violation, an individual's report

3. For an example of decision under multiple standards, see Victor G. Rosen-
blum, "How To Get into TV: The Federal Communications Commission and
Miami's Channel 10," in Alan F. Westin, *The Uses of Power* (New York: Harcourt, Brace & World, Inc., 1962), pp. 173–228.

of income on which his tax is based, or the specifications and bids from which a contract award is determined. Much of the process of bureaucratization and elimination of favoritism is dependent on the perfection of the records. Beyond this, it is important to have an institutional process that ensures that the record is the basis of decision, either as developed on the form or by later deliberations. Normally, there is some kind of check and balance system within administration to ensure adherence to rules and regard for the records. For example, there is in the Internal Revenue Service an elaborate process of internal review and of appeal from one level to another. Other agencies have various kinds of audits or cross-checks.

The third means is to seek judgment by persons who will act expertly and impersonally. This may be a complement to the other means, the application of rule and the decision on the records being entrusted to persons who are trained to act impersonally. Also, the submergence of decisions in administrative process will force impersonality, both in the attitudes of particular persons and through the institutional process of group deliberation and internal checks and balances. The dependence upon impersonality is greater, however, where judgment is not fully guided by the compulsions of law and the identity or similarity of factual situations. Examples of the effort to get expert, impersonal decision are: the use of lawyers' talents in regulatory administration; the use of scientists' talents in such agencies as the Patent Office, the Food and Drug Administration, and the Bureau of Standards; and the use of trained case workers in welfare administration.

Although departures are sometimes made from these bureaucratic devices, there is seldom complete departure from them in the administrative state. There is, for example, departure from professional administration in the jury system. But the jury is hedged and limited in many ways, such as the charge of the judge on the law, the right of appeal on legal issues, and the setting of penalties in most jurisdictions by the judge. There are many who believe it should be hedged and limited more than it is, at least in some types of causes. An example of departure from strict rule of law and professional administration exists in selective service administration. But several things may be noted. The system of administration was probably adopted initially because of the need for a convenient, localized system of administration. The reputed advantage of a decision by a "committee of neighbors" is a myth created to justify continuance of the system.[4] National rules have progressively narrowed the discretion of the lay boards, so that over nine-tenths of the judgments can be made by clerks, with reference to the boards for automatic approval. Moreover, the National Advisory Commission on Selective Service, appointed by the President, recommended that the system of administration be reorganized on the basis of the principle of rule of law, that is, that national rules should be expanded to prevent different standards from being applied to the same factual situations in different jurisdictions.[5] Even these examples from the jury system and selective service show there is normally an attempt to provide, wholly or partially, that microdecisions will be the same for all in like circumstances.

In sum, the primary route to reduction of micropolitics is bureaucratic administration—administration according to rule, immersed in process, and protected by impersonal judgment. On the plane of microdecisions we seek to introduce the advantages of the methods of the administrative state.

There are, however, practical limitations on the program-

4. Roscoe C. Martin has discussed government by friends and neighbors with some care in his *Grass Roots* (University, Alabama: University of Alabama Press, 1957); see also Emmette S. Redford, *Field Administration of Wartime Rationing* (Washington, D.C.: Superintendent of Documents, 1947), Chapters 2 and 10.

5. Report of the National Advisory Committee on Selective Service, *In Pursuit of Equity: Who Serves When Not All Serve* (Washington, D.C.: Superintendent of Documents, 1967), p. 5.

ming of microdecisions for bureaucratic administration. They arise from the fact that in spite of all efforts, micropolitics—exercised through strategic positions that provide access for some and not for others—will invade the arenas of public decision. I shall note here three subforms of micropolitics that can invade administration.

One is the politics of association. There is the hazard that bureaucratic institutions will develop political connections of their own that threaten their impartiality in microdecisions. Students of the subject may, for illustration, read the case study on battery additives. The Bureau of Standards, which we expect to be a paragon of virtue, was shown to have close connections with a trade association that could bias its judgment, or cause suspicion of such bias, concerning an application from a person whose interests were opposed to that of the association.[6] The case also illustrates another kind of bias—the bias toward decision on the basis of the kind of data familiar to a given professional group. The decision was made on laboratory tests in the face of claims by the applicant that field tests by users of his product showed different results from those obtained in the laboratory. The lesson is that specialized agencies develop an affinity for the methodologies of the groups with which they are constantly associated, and of which they are indeed often a part. This will no doubt usually be an advantage, but it also presents a hazard.

The politics of association is most patently revealed in the communities of interest developed between those who award and those who receive grants and contracts in our scientific, military, and educational administrations. A kind of court politics—that between professionals in granting and those in receiving institutions—gives advantage to those occupying strategic positions in the inner circle of professional relation-

6. See Samuel A. Lawrence, *The Battery Additive Controversy* (Indianapolis: Bobbs-Merrill Company, 1962, No. 68 of the Inter-University Case Committee Studies).

ships. The old-court politics formed by the association of city bosses and contractors has been undermined, in part by the programming of microdecisions through the requirement of competitive bidding. In the new-court politics, discretion in the awarding of grants and contracts is wide, and the rules against participation in the awards by those who have interests as recipients are often weak defenses against communities of interest.

The second subform of micropolitics is the politics of external influence. The President, party officials, members of Congress, and association executives are the main centers through which superior access to decision-making forums may be obtained. In regulatory administration, as in judicial administration, there is now an accepted standard on improper conduct: when a matter is set down for decision on a record it is improper for anyone to try to influence the decision except by facts and arguments openly placed on the record. The principle has been confirmed in rules of agencies, some of which provide that any communication—written or oral, coming from any source to any member of the agency— relating to the matter under consideration must be disclosed in the record.

Unfortunately, even with the tradition of independence for regulatory agencies, it is not easy to develop an equal protection against micropolitics in the consideration of decisions not required to be made on a record. Examples of such decisions are those on whether to initiate an investigation, whether to prosecute, or whether to accept a settlement before issuance of a complaint. Since Sherman Adams's resignation as assistant to President Eisenhower (following revelations of his contacts with two regulatory commissions on behalf of a friend), Presidents have made special efforts to avoid contacts with commissions on such matters by members of their staffs. Congressmen, however, do not feel bound by the rule of abstinence with respect to regulatory agencies. Moreover, there has been little attention given to the problem of proper relationships of the President and Congress to other agencies on microdecisions. Yet the principle established for microdecisions in regulatory administration is, I submit, the appropriate guide for other microdecisions applicable to individuals or single firms: these types of decisions should not be made under political influence, particularly through strategic centers in which large political power can be aggregated.

There are, I hasten to add, issues concerning application of or departure from the principle. When, for instance, does that which on its face is a microdecision become a macrodecision, i.e. a decision with general effects extending far beyond those of the interests of the individual or company immediately affected? Even in regulatory administration Congress has made some exceptions to the general principle that may have justification: the President must approve or disapprove applications for foreign air transportation--presumably because of the potential effects on our relations with foreign countries, or the suspension of a securities exchange from doing business--presumably because of the wide effects of such a decision. And when do a series of decisions or failures to act on matters affecting particular individuals or firms justify the attention of Congress or the President? When, in other words, do microdecisions become reason for consideration of the rules being applied or of the system of administration?

A third subform of micropolitics is built into the system of decision making. This is reflected most clearly in the participation of members of Congress in the making of microdecisions of interest to particular communities. I find in a report of the Senate Committee on Appropriations dated July 11, 1967, the naming of 30 new and the expansion of 67 old agricultural research centers. It is not surprising that contests arise over such locations, and that in the report of the conference committee it is noted that one of the new centers—a grassland research laboratory—was awarded to a city in the district of the chairman of the Committee on Agriculture of the House of Representatives, a different location from that recommended by the Senate Committee. The most familiar area of congressional participation in microdecisions is, of course, river projects. On those constructed by the Army Engineers, Congress participates at three stages: a request that a study of the feasibility of the project be made by the Army Engineers, an authorization for the project subsequent to a report that it is feasible, and one or more appropriations for its construction.

The efforts to contain micropolitics on river projects is highly instructive. Congress has recognized the need for means of differentiating among projects and protecting the general interests against excessive authorizations and appropriations. The safeguards it has created are the usual ones in the administrative state: to establish a rule and require administrative process. The substantive rule, embodied in statute, is that no project will be approved unless there is a ratio of benefits to costs of at least one to one. The administrative process encompasses a study of feasibility, a finding on the ratio of benefits to costs, and a recommendation by the Army Engineers. But these devices have not eliminated micropolitics from the decisions. For one thing, the use of rule is incomplete. As applied there are biases toward overstatement of benefits and understatement of costs. Moreover, the determinations are inconclusive because many more projects meet the requirements of the rule than can be authorized. Second, politics engulfs the whole process. A web of political relationships keeps the Army Engineers dependent upon the related program committees and appropriations subcommittees of Congress, and the decisions in Congress reflect the bargaining strength of members.

It is interesting, however, that all proposals for strengthening the safeguards suggest either a hardening of the rule or more independence in the administrative process. As for the rule, the usual proposals are that it be applied with stricter regard for professional standards, that the benefit-cost ratio be higher, or that priorities be established among those projects meeting the minimum standard. As for the administrative process, the Bureau of the Budget has inserted itself into the process of recommendations, but without much effect. Successive groups, such as the first and second Hoover commissions, have made recommendations looking toward an analysis of projects by some unit more independent of congressional influence than the Army Engineers. The suggestion for the item veto for the President assumes that the exercise of the veto will be based on independent analysis of the projects.[7]

It cannot be reasonably expected that micropolitics can be eliminated from the consideration of community projects. The interests of communities are high-quantity interests realizable only through public action, and such interests are likely to find some means of influence on any forum in which the power of decision is located. Moreover, members of Congress have a high personal stake in retaining their own participation in decisions. Gaining benefits for the folks back home is good re-election technique.

Yet the reduction of micropolitics through the extension of use of the devices of the administrative state is crucial to equal consideration of community interests and protection of general interests. On the one hand, the federal larder grows in size and in kinds of benefits available to communities. Installations of the armed forces, science projects, Job Corp locations, model-city and rent-subsidy selections, and other kinds of projects create vast opportunities for differential advantage. On the other hand, there is a growing intrusiveness by Congress into administrative matters that enlarges

7. For fuller analysis of the politics of river projects, see Arthur Maass, *Muddy Waters: The Army Engineers and the Nation's Rivers* (Cambridge, Mass.: Harvard University Press, 1951), and Otto Eckstein, *Water-Resource Development: The Economics of Project Evaluation* (Cambridge, Mass.: Harvard University Press, 1958).

the opportunities of members to serve their communities on microdecisions. One way of making microdecisions is through the politics of bargaining and influence. This cannot be eliminated; the devices of the administrative state offer the only hope for its reduction.

At the same time, the introduction of the methods of bureaucracy into microdecisions carries with it some definite hazards. There is danger that the administrative state will not operate with the effectiveness we expect of it, or that it may have by-products we dislike. One hazard is that of inefficiency. Students of public administration may read, for illustration of this hazard, a case study of the Patent Office as it operated in the 'forties.[8] Inefficiency in operations created delays in the processing of applications for patents that prevented realization of patent benefits to persons and firms legally entitled to them. Technical inefficiency is, however, probably the least of the problems of bureaucracy in this day of efficiency studies and management expertness within administration.

Another hazard is that bureaus will develop insensitivities to human needs that create rule tropism beyond what is necessary for program effectiveness or what will be accepted by people subject to administration. Fear of purely bureaucratic or professional administration is evidenced in the most traditional and elaborate of all systems of administration— the administration of justice. We have used the jury system to prevent professional insensitivity in microdecisions intimately affecting human rights and interests. We occasionally adopt other techniques of nonprofessional administration in new programs of administration.

The third hazard is that, in spite of the devices for eliminating or minimizing micropolitics, access to administrative agencies making microdecisions will still be unequal. All the formal arrangements may still not prevent the police from dealing more sympathetically with the sons of the rich and

8. In Harold Stein, ed., *Public Administration and Policy Development: A Case Book* (New York: Harcourt, Brace and Co., 1952), pp. 1–13.

powerful than with the sons of the poor. The devices we have mentioned do not guarantee access to all. Costs of effective access may be too high. Dean Landis found in a study of regulatory administration that the costs of administrative justice were too high to be incurred by many firms.[9] This, however, affects fewer persons than some of the other costs of access. There is, for example, the shameful lack of equality that has existed for centuries in the positions of rich and poor before our courts. Nothing could be more important to a man than effective access to the deciding tribunal when he is accused of crime. Yet society long paid for proficiency in the prosecution of the case against a man but did not provide for proficiency in the presentation of his defense. Judicial administration has been glorified as application of rules by impersonal judges, but of what value is this if a man does not have effective access to the tribunal? Moreover, the poor may lack knowledge that law and administration have been created to provide benefits for them, or may be unaware of the procedures available to obtain these benefits. There must be many a scalped borrower of money who does not know that there are official agencies to protect him from such scalping.

This phase of the discussion may be concluded with several propositions. First, there are means available in an administered society for reducing the incidence and effectiveness of micropolitics. Second, we can be reasonably hopeful that in the most micro of microdecisions, those affecting particular persons or firms, we can protect the equalitarian ideal against micropolitics. Third, in the case of community interests the protections will be less effective, but means of partial protection are available. Fourth, the greatest hazards of the administrative state may be, not its subversion by micropolitics, but the failure of the macropolitical system when making macrodecisions to take the steps that are necessary

9. James M. Landis, *Report on Regulatory Agencies to the President-Elect* (Committee Print, Committee on the Judiciary, U.S. Senate, 86th Cong., 2d Sess., 1960), p. 10.

to humanize administration and provide effective access for all. So important is this aspect of our subject that I shall discuss it separately (Chapter VI).

In Chapter II it was said that the basic feature of the administrative state is the concentration of decision making in strategic positions within organizations with program specializations. Also, the interactions among strategic official centers and between these and strategic power centers exerting influence on them were noted. In Chapter III a system (the red-line system) of interaction between positions within the executive branch and Congress was described. It is time now to examine the fusion of these factors in subsystems of political administration. Illustrations will be given of the interactions among strategic centers of program specialization in the executive branch, the Congress, and the power groups on the outside. The implications for the democratic ideal will be analyzed.

In 1939 Ernest Griffith introduced an analysis of this aspect of politics and administration with these words:

> One cannot live in Washington for long without being conscious that it has whirlpools or centers of activity focusing on particular problems. . . . It is my opinion that ordinarily the relationship among these men—legislators, administrators, lobbyists, scholars—who are interested in a common problem is a much more real relationship than the relationship between congressmen generally or between administrators generally.[10]

Building on this theme and looking for "key participants in special areas of the American public-policy-making process," Leiper Freeman in 1955 found that the over-all political setting promoted "considerable autonomy for bureaus, com-

10. Ernest S. Griffith, *The Impasse of Democracy* (New York: Harrison-Hilton Books, Inc., 1939), p. 182.

mittees, and interest groups." The result was the development of "policy-making subsystems formed by the interactions of the leaders" of these three. A subsystem tended "to have a decisive quality of its own," the chief participants interacting with and to one another "to some degree independently of the larger political world of which the system is a part." [11]

Freeman studied the interaction of the Bureau of Indian Affairs, congressional committees, and interests groups during approximately twenty years following the advent of the New Deal. His discussion reflected, on the whole, disunities within the system. There was lack of unity in each of the three types of participants. Represented among groups seeking to influence policy were nonclientele groups with a philosophical orientation and tending to support the New Dealist attitudes of the Indian Bureau. Also represented were local, material-minded groups who sought influence particularly through the American Indian Federation and found a sympathetic ear in the Senate. In the Congress there was lack of unity in the positions of the committees on Indian affairs, the appropriations subcommittees, and the investigating committees (usually subcommittees of the committees on Indian affairs). Even in the bureau, the chief found some difficulty in maintaining unity of position among employees. There was, moreover, continuing tension between the bureau and congressmen. The membership of the committees on Indian affairs was drawn overwhelmingly from western or Indian-minority-populated states. This explained their "frequent tendencies to work counter to a Bureau that promoted the interests of Indian minorities in the face of objections by local whites." [12] There was a running battle between the Bureau and the chairman of the House appropriations subcommittee.

In general, Freeman believed that the relationships be-

11. J. Leiper Freeman, *The Political Process: Executive-Bureau–Legislative Committee Relations* (Garden City, N.Y.: Doubleday & Company, Inc., 1955), pp. 1, 14–15, 33.
12. Ibid. p. 51.

tween the bureau and the committee tended to be institutionalized and depersonalized and to grow out of different
orientations and role requirements of committee members
and bureau leaders. In general, the bureau was also sensi-
tized to committee positions, and the likely tendency of the
system as a whole was toward moderation of conflicts.[13] The
system, moreover, did not operate with complete autonomy.
For example, bureau chiefs sought support from the executive hierarchy, and congressional investigating committees
tried to gain the attention of the same hierarchy and of a
larger public audience than ordinarily gave attention to Indian affairs.

A study of the subsystem for river developments by Arthur
Maass emphasized the unity within the subsystem as it existed
in 1949. The Corps of Engineers regarded itself as directly
responsible "to the legislature as a body, and more particularly to certain legislative committees and to individual members of the legislature." [14] The Corps, the committees, and
members of Congress, all reflected the local interests in river
development projects. The most important interest group
organization was the National Rivers and Harbors Congress,
whose function was to unify local interest groups, the Congress, and the Corps of Engineers. It drew its membership
from " 'local interests' (state and local officials, local industrial
and trade organizations, contractors); the United States Congress (Representatives and Senators are honorary members);
and the Corps of Engineers (Officers of the Corps engaged in
rivers and harbors work are all ex officio members)." [15] Both
of the latter two groups actively participated in the proceedings of the Rivers and Harbors Congress. This interest association not only has included members of Congress, but has
elected strategically located members of Congress to its presi
dency, vice presidencies, and chairmanship of the board. The

13. Ibid. pp. 63 and 67.
14. Maass, *Muddy Waters,* p. 63.
15. Ibid. pp. 45–46.

association considers and recommends particular projects for authorization by Congress, usually approving the recommendations of the Corps of Engineers. Maass describes the efforts, relatively unsuccessful, of the superstructure of the executive branch to break into this tight subsystem.

I have studied the subsystem for promotion and regulation of domestic commercial civil aviation. Part of the study was an analysis of all that happened with respect to civil aviation in the Eighty-fifth Congress.[16] In general, I found a more complex system than is portrayed in Freeman's description of Indian affairs and one in which great concurrencies, as well as large differences of interest, are apparent. It is also a system with high concentration of decision making but nevertheless with much less cohesiveness than that prevailing in the tightly structured system Maass described.

The foundation of the system was laid in a remarkable consensus registered in the Civil Aeronautics Act of 1938. The consensus was for promotion of aviation transport through protection of safety and development of a certificated sound air-transport industry, subsidized to the extent necessary to provide adequate service. The consensus reflected the concordant views of a nascent industry, the Administration, congressional leaders, and a trusted transportation expert who garnered from his experience in railroad regulation the guidelines for a new industry. It set the boundaries within which government policy and structure and industry policy have been developed. Among other things it sought to delegate to administrative structures the microdecisions concerning licensing of pilots, granting of routes, and determination

16. Emmette S. Redford, "A Case Analysis of Congressional Activity: Civil Aviation, 1957–58," *The Journal of Politics,* Vol. XXII (May 1960), pp. 228–58. The discussion here is based also on two other parts of the study: "The Significance of Belief Patterns in Economic Regulation," *The Western Political Quarterly,* Vol. XIV (September 1961), pp. 13–25, and *Congress Passes the Federal Aviation Act of 1958* (Indianapolis: Bobbs-Merrill Company, 1961, Number 62 of Inter-University Case Committee Studies). The text describes the situation as it existed at the time these pieces were written.

of subsidy rates to companies. Yet between the basic assumptions and rules of policy and the microdecisions was left an area of discretion for administrative agencies and of issues for consideration in Congress. Although these issues have sometimes erupted into macropolitics, they have been largely determined by actors within the subsystem.

The heart of the subsystem is formed by the primary working centers for civil aviation, which may be considered to form a triangle. At the administrative corner of the triangle are the Civil Aeronautics Board and the Federal Aviation Agency, the former responsible for economic regulation and promotion, the latter for safety and for physical promotion through grants for airport construction. At the congressional corner are the committees on commerce and the appropriations subcommittees. Within the commerce committees there are subcommittees: in the House one on transportation and communication, in the Senate one on aviation. Within the subcommittees a small number of persons are strategically located for influence on policy. The Senate Aviation Subcommittee has only five members and has been chaired since its formation in 1955 by Senator Monroney. He has the most strategic position on aviation policy in public or private structure. It is perhaps not too much to say that he is the nation's chief co-ordinator of aviation policy and can exercise a virtual veto on any program proposals. At the industry corner are a large number of associations representing general aviation, the commercial industry, airline pilots, and other interests. Strongest of these on industry matters is the Air Transport Association, representing certificated companies. Its long-time president, Mr. Stuart Tipton, testifies at nearly every committee hearing affecting aviation, and with his associates he is in constant contact with all the important centers through which aviation policy is influenced. He too is an important influence in the co-ordination of aviation policy.

Notwithstanding these concentrations of opportunities for

influence from strategic positions, many factors limit the occupants of the positions. Tipton, heading a confederation of companies with differing interests, can take a position only on matters on which the industry is united. Monroney must balance the great variety of interests—the "nonskeds" and the certificated carriers, the local-service and trunk carriers, the military and the civil industry, general aviation and commercial aviation; and in these and other balances must also reflect the interests of communities in more air service. The appropriations subcommittees must balance the claims for safety against the rapidly mounting costs of providing it. Also, other committees, such as those on government operations and the judiciary committees, will repeatedly get into aviation matters. Moreover, the aviation subsystem will sometimes overlap and come into conflict with other subsystems. Twice in the Eighty-fifth Congress—on MATS-civil air transport and on the controls of the new Federal Aviation Agency over the military—the members of Congress dealing with commercial aviation and those dealing with defense came into conflict, and compromises had to be made between the rival sets of interests. In addition, there were many conflicts between CAB and congressional committees and between CAB and other administrative agencies; there was also a long-standing conflict between Monroney and the agency which until 1958 was responsible for safety.

Finally, aviation matters sometimes spill over into macropolitics. During the Eighty-fifth Congress President Eisenhower vetoed a bill for extension of airport subsidies and was forced to choose between dropping his plans for a transportation department and supporting a federal aviation agency. His representatives and Monroney had to compromise many differences on the Federal Aviation Act. A couple of bad accidents shifted Monroney's desire for a new and stronger agency for safety protection from subsystem politics to a level where it concerned the President, all members of Congress, and the general press.

My studies of civil aviation support some general statements relative to our inquiry on democracy. The policy-making process sometimes forges general consensus into law, as in the Civil Aeronautics Act and the chief provisions of the Federal Aviation Act; but usually it reconciles conflicting and complementary interests outside and also positions taken within the government. Second, most of the issues will be mediated in subsystems by persons in strategic positions. Third, high-quantity interests have superior opportunities for access through association representatives. But, finally, other interests do get representation. Scarcely any transportation interest has not had access through hearings or other means to the policy makers. In the Eighty-fifth Congress, the weaker party in the airline industry—the nonskeds—won a fairly substantial victory, and the diffused interests of the public were represented in Monroney's battles for stronger safety protection and continuance of airport subsidies to communities. In a study of a particular case in the CAB (the no-show —over sales agreement) I have shown also that the diffused interests of consumers are not overlooked in that agency.[17]

Conclusions

There is probably some kind of subsystem for every major activity of the government. We need much more study on the representation of interests in these subsystems, particularly in the arenas of international, defense and science policy. Four propositions tend, however, to be substantiated by the existing evidence that has been presented in a variety of studies.

First, subsystems provide stability for existing equilibriums among interests. In Indian affairs Freeman thought there was a tendency toward moderate policies that did not move radically toward the rival positions of contending parties.

17. Chapter VI in Emmette S. Redford, *The Regulatory Process: With Illustrations from Commercial Aviation* (Austin: The University of Texas Press, to be published in 1969).

The discussion of river development projects shows how the interaction among strategic centers insulates against external invasion of an existing system. It is clear also that the consensus on values registered in the Civil Aeronautics Act of 1938 has not been disturbed. One is impressed as he reads through nearly thirty years of congressional hearings on civil aviation by the interstitial quality of issues repeatedly and laboriously considered. Corroborative evidence from other areas is mountainous. The ability of subsystems to absorb attacks, to prolong discussions through numerous inquiries, and to protect existing equilibriums is enormous.

The reasons for this are clear. There is continuity in strategic positions. These tend to remain the same, and their occupants serve for long periods and are socialized into the roles they play. New occupants of these positions are assimilated or made ineffective. On this there is no dissimilarity between occupants of congressional and of administrative positions—seniority and socialization in committees have the same results as tenure in bureaus. And on commissions the sheer volume of work, the dependence on staff, and the sharing of responsibility with other commissioners absorb, or lead to the resignation of, imaginative and bold new members.

The evidence shows that we must abandon hope and fear of radical innovation through the instruments of coadministration in Congress and administrative agencies. The revolution that has produced and continues to produce the administered society lies in forces outside the subsystems that to a substantial extent form the administrative state.

Second, subsystems provide continuous access and superior opportunities for influence to high-quantity, aggregated interests. High-quantity interests in Indian affairs are protected through an association, congressional committees, and bureau sensitivity to their strength. High-quantity industry interests in commercial aviation are protected by the ubiquitous access of their associations, and high-quantity community interests in river development by multiple access through associations, congressmen, and the politically minded Corps of Engineers. Here, too, the corroborative evidence from other areas is mountainous.

There is danger, however, that the significant fact stated in this second proposition will lead to distorted or exaggerated conclusions. There is much talk about captive agencies, and there should be some about captive congressional committees. But access for high-quantity interests does not necessarily mean that agencies or committees are completely captured by any single interest, for both agencies and committees often have multiple clienteles. It used to be said that the Interstate Commerce Commission was railroad-minded,[18] but the railroad companies have struggled for legislation that they thought was necessary to counteract fancied motor-carrier favoritism in the commission's rate policies. The fact is that the ICC can survive only by maintaining a "moving balance" among a variety of interests. My examination of the interests—even those that are aggregated in associations—shows almost indescribable diversities that Senator Monroney, the CAB, and the Federal Aviation Agency must take into account. Freeman has suggested the "possibility that in subsystems the influence of groups expressing certain orientations waxes and wanes and shifts its focus from one part of the subsystem to another. . . ."[19]

All this is pertinent to democracy. Subsystems are arenas for adjustment of contesting interests. They may overbalance the results in favor of high-quantity, aggregated interests, but they cannot avoid the necessity of mediating such interests by giving some "loaves and fishes" to each. It is further significant for democracy that the roles prescribed for administrative agencies by macropolitical action set limits upon the concessions they can make to particular interests. This ac-

18. See, for example, Samuel P. Huntington, "The Marasmus of the ICC: The Commission, the Railroads, and the Public Interest," *Yale Law Journal,* Vol. LXII (December 1952), pp. 171–225.
19. *The Political Process,* p. 60.

counts for the appeals that high-quantity interests frequently make from the subsystems to macropolitics.

Third, subsystems provide some access and representation to interests that are not dominant. While the systems tend to maintain the interests represented in the existing equilibriums, they still provide some access to other interests. And those which find the door to one forum shut may turn to another door, for the subsystems provide multiple channels of access. Occasional victories are won by even the normally excluded. Note again the example of the quite substantial victory of the nonskeds against the opposition of the certificated airline industry in legislation passed by the Eighty-fifth Congress. And again and again it must be emphasized that roles prescribed in organic legislation for administrative agencies provide some representation for distributed interests.

Fourth, substantial changes in the balances among interests served by subsystems can be expected to occur only through macropolitical intervention that modifies the rules and roles operating in the systems. Subsystem actors operate within the confines of existing organic rules and institutional roles that delineate the system of which they are a part. They lack both the formal position and the political strength to change materially by their own efforts alone the established allocation of benefits among competing and concurring interests. They are especially weak with respect to changes that are opposed by high-quantity interest aggregations.

A recent administrator of the agency responsible for promotion of American flagships in foreign trade was greatly disturbed because, although the government subsidized substantially the flagship dollar, we still had a declining merchant marine. He repeatedly inquired in informal consultations: What can we do about it? How can we promote the assumed diffused interest of the American people in an adequate American shipping industry? The difficulty was that he, like many other administrators, was boxed in by intricately interlaced, high-quantity labor and business interests.

My own response to his inquiry was that no initiatives would be fruitful unless there was, first, a journalistic exposure by an Ida Tarbell or a Ralph Nader and, second, a willingness on the part of the President to expend some of his scarce political capital in bold support of a concrete proposal for change of the rules. A subsystem actor is helpless to bring about radical change unless the issues are raised into the arena of macropolitics.

Appeal from subsystem to macropolitics may originate from within or from outside the subsystem. The passage of the Federal Aviation Act shows how a subsystem actor, in this instance Senator Monroney, struggled within the subsystem for stronger rules and roles in safety protection and then was able, because of two accidents, to marshal support from outside the subsystem for amendment of the governing statute. But more often presidential leadership supplies the initiative for substantial subsystem change.

What, finally, are the conclusions that can be stated about democracy in the subsystems of the administered society? First, they are themselves imperfect instruments of democratic government. The roles prescribed by macropolitical action make subsystems serve to some extent as conveyor belts for continued representation of certain interests that have prevailed in the macropolitical process. Beyond this they are mediators of interests within the areas of autonomy that develop for them. In this double behavior of loyalty to prescribed role and mediation of interests, democracy may be impaired by the superior access of some interests and the under access of others; but the multiple points of access in our national politics provide some opportunity for any interest that is prepared to assert itself. Second, there are opportunities for appeal to macropolitical action through which the roles reflected in subsystem action may be modified to some extent. The strength and weakness of the macropolitical system for the discharge of its appeal function will be discussed in the next chapter.

V

The Macropolitical System

MACROPOLITICS WAS DEFINED earlier as the politics that arises when the community at large and the leaders of the government as a whole are brought into the discussion and determination of issues. The distinguishing factor is the breadth of involvement. Because of the two elements in the definition there are niceties of distinction, but these need not obscure the main point. It is possible for a top leader, even the President, to get involved in a micropolitical issue, or be drawn into a subsystem discussion, without the matters at issue ever engaging sufficient attention to command macropolitical concern. Generally, however, it is the breadth or potential breadth of attention that determines the agenda of top officials. The questions forced upward out of subsystems are normally matters that raise broader issues and concern wider interests than can be determined within them. When the policies of the police department break on the front pages of newspapers and into discussions in the city council, when issues of higher education engage the attention of the governor and of those who apportion funds among state functions, and when the affairs of national intelligence agencies erupt into public discussion or the President gives his attention to large foreign and domestic issues, then we have politics in the wider arena defined here as macropolitics.

Chart III displays in two concentric circles the nature of the macropolitical system. The outer circle shows the input

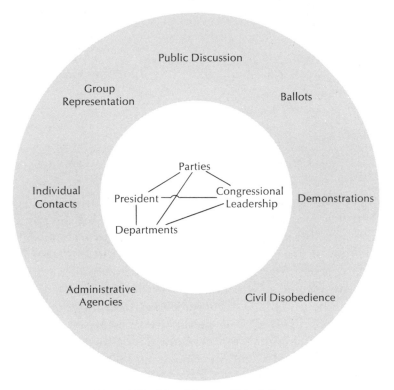

Chart III   The Macropolitical System

factors in macropolitics. Through public discussion, ballots, individual contacts, group representation, action by administrative agencies, demonstrations, and civil disobedience demands on the governmental system are made known. The inner circle shows the instruments of conversion of demands into policy and action in the macropolitical system. These are the national parties, the President, the department heads, and the congressional leaders.

There is, of course, yet another kind of input, namely, the environmental factors that press issues into the system. Episodes (such as the Cuban missile crisis), a technological development, a shortage in a basic resource, a failure in or threat to the economic system, a change in belief patterns, and other like factors, generate new activity in the system.

In this chapter, attention will be concentrated on the inner circle, emphasizing the functions, instruments, and implications for democracy of the central institutions of the macropolitical system. There are three themes in the discussion. The first: There are functions of vast importance to be performed in the macropolitical institutions. The second: These institutions are poorly organized for the performance of their inevitable functions. The third: There are factors of strength and weakness in the realization of the democratic ideal through these institutions.

THE FUNCTIONS OF THE MACROPOLITICAL SYSTEM

It has been assumed in traditional democratic theory that the representatives of electorates in the macropolitical institutions should have supremacy over administrative institutions and, hence, over any subsystems which develop around these. This was referred to earlier as overhead democracy.

The assumption in theory might be supported by three kinds of reasoning. The first would be by argument that the macropolitical institutions are more representative than the subsystem institutions. In view of the importance of the assumption, it is unfortunate that there has been little empirical analysis to test it. Norton Long has argued that because of its origins, income level, and associations, our civil service is more representative than Congress.[1] Others might argue that the channels of access to the multiple centers of influence in subsystems are superior to those in the macropolitical system—because of their number, their constant and more ready availability, or the intensity of consideration of issues within the subsystems. While organized, high-quantity

1. Norton E. Long, "Bureaucracy and Constitutionalism," *The American Political Science Review*, Vol. XLVI (September 1952), pp. 808–18.

interests seem to have great influence within subsystems, they may have strong influence in macropolitics as well. Further, there is the constant quandary of democracy as to the proper balance between high-quantity and low-quantity interests. The American people have often shown that they placed greater trust, for the long pull, in subsystems than in macropolitics. Witness, as examples, the efforts to give independence to regulatory functions, to state administrative agencies, and to the local educational function.

On the issue of representativeness it is possible to state a proposition, a corollary, and an hypothesis. The proposition is this: the macropolitical system provides channels of access not otherwise available for interests in the society. The corollary is: interests that fail to gain influence in the subsystems may obtain it through the macropolitical system. The hypothesis is: diffused unfulfilled interests, quantity interests, and newly asserted interests will find their greatest opportunities to challenge existing equilibriums of interests in the macropolitical system. Any of these three, or two or all in combination, will attest the importance of macropolitical representation in a democracy.

The second line of reasoning in that public actors in administrative systems can claim legitimacy for their activities only if they are authorized by an external source—and in a democracy, only if that source can claim responsibility to the people. They must be able to claim that they have official roles delegated to them, that they do not act personally by usurpation. They may argue that definition of official role cannot determine absolutely their action, asserting constitutional, cultural, or higher-law values not reflected in the act of delegation; but they cannot avoid the necessity of an external authorization of their position. This will be essential for acceptance of their roles by society.

The third kind of reasoning is deterministic. The argument is that in the nature of things there are functions that must be performed in a macropolitical system. Whatever arguments might be advanced for decentralization to subsystems, there are—by virtue both of the constitutional system and of necessity—functions that must be performed in the macropolitical system. Seven of these are distinguishable.

First, choices must be made on programs, and on rules and roles with respect to these. Government, for example, protects investors by choices in favor of a program for regulation of security issues, rules requiring prospectuses, and creation of roles for actors in the Securities Exchange Commission. Or it protects the aged by choices in favor of medicare and medicaid programs, rules for each, and roles for the Social Security Administration, for the Public Health Service, and for co-operating state agencies. If the basic programs, the basic rules, and the primary roles are to be substantially expanded or modified, then this too requires macropolitical action. In sum, overhead decisions bring into existence the administrative state, generate its subsystems, and set the bounds of their operations.

Second, resources must be allocated among subsystems and decisions must be made on how these resources will be obtained. If it were possible to make every program self-sustaining and to allow each administrative agency to arrange for this as it could, then allocative decisions could be delegated. But most government programs are not self-sustaining and their purposes would be defeated if any attempt were made to make them so. Hence tax and borrowing decisions must be made, and the money obtained must be allocated by budget decisions. Much of the history of the rise of representative (and of democratic) government is connected with the development of macropolitical institutions to make these fiscal decisions. At times, moreover, other types of allocative decisions may have to be made. Manpower or materials shortages may call for limitations on their use by public agencies. This was true, for example, in World War II when agencies had to compete for allocations of manpower and scarce materials, as well as for money.

Third, there is a personnel function which requires attention at the highest level. Decisions must be made on the manning of agencies. At least decisions must be made on nuclear personnel—on one or more persons to initiate or maintain a program. It is possible that the initial nucleus of personnel could be delegated some power to arrange both for additional personnel and for succession of personnel. But it cannot be expected that those who establish programs and allocate resources to them will not be continuously interested in the manning of the programs.

The above functions relate to the establishment, maintenance, and scope of subsystems. The activities described create, sustain, and man specialized organizations for continuing functions. They thus have a constituent, or organic, quality. They may, however, draw the macropolitical institutions into quite specific determinations. This result is accentuated by the next three functions.

Fourth, there is an appellate function. Those who are dissatisfied with the services rendered by or with the equilibriums maintained within subsystems will search for appellate jurisdictions. They will not always be satisfied by opportunities for appeal within the subsystems or to the judiciary, and will press their claims in the macropolitical political system. Similarly, those who desire the maintenance or expansion of subsystem activity will reach upward for support, and for defense against attack, to macropolitical institutions. Moreover, issues arise in the subsystems that are of such large import to affected interests that they move upward into the macropolitical institutions.

Fifth, there are issues that are elevated immediately into the macropolitical structure. These often create what can be broadly referred to as the crisis function. The bombing of Pearl Harbor, the invasion of South Korea, the Cuban missile confrontation, the steel-price increase of 1962, deadlocks in labor-management negotiations, and riots in the cities, are examples of events that throw decisions immediately and inescapably into the macropolitical arena.

Sixth, there is a co-ordinative function. As the complexity of the functions of the administrative state expands, there develop interlockings, mutual interdependencies, and conflicts among agency activities, and indeed among subsystems. While defense, diplomacy, research and development, and domestic programs of various sorts are in large measure structured separately, they must repeatedly, indeed almost continuously, be co-ordinated. Even programs that appear to have unity of purpose, but that are in fact categories of varied programs with specialized purposes—as in education and welfare—cannot now be structured in a single department or bureau. Job training, for example, is related to the general function of the Department of Labor as well as to that of the Office of Education. It is not possible to organize administration in such a way as to avoid participation across subsystem lines. Moreover, while co-operative arrangements among agencies performing related functions, and mutual awareness among them of their separate interests, will produce some co-ordination and compose some differences, a superstructure will be required to mediate conflicts, overcome resistances, and carry co-ordination still further.

Finally, there is a review function. I am not speaking normatively of a need for a review function, but objectively of the results of the other functions that have been outlined. It is inevitable that those who create functions and rules and roles, who allocate resources, and who must hear appeals, will be interested in the methods and results of the systems they create and sustain. Thus those who tax and allocate funds will be interested in conservation, and fidelity in the use, of funds. It is not accidental that historically the interest of legislative bodies in England and the United States in taxes and appropriations was paralleled by interest in audits or that in recent years there has been much interest within legislative bodies in economy and efficiency, as well as in fidelity, in the use of money. Thus, also, it is not accidental that investigation and review have been functions of the macropolitical superstructure.

In sum, an overhead structure will exist for organic, allocative, manning, appellate, crisis, co-ordinative, and review functions. This does not mean either that the overhead structure can assume complete direction and supervision or that it will operate with full unity of purpose. There are identifiable features of the operation of the overhead that determine its scope and quality. First, overhead intervention is selective. The continuing public business of society lies in the subsystems. The superstructure does not allow for continuous attention to all, or for attention to much, that is happening in the administrative state. And the occupants of the structure will not desire to intervene when this will mean some loss of their political capital. Selection results, therefore, by avoidance as well as by intervention.

Second, the macropolitical structure will be under pressure to perform a range of functions, extending from momentary attention and action on specific issues to synoptic planning and general policy determination. Society will expect the macropolitical structure to be prepared to handle appeals and crises that rise to the top floor of the public edifice, but it will expect also that drawing boards for solutions of policy issues will be located on that floor. Even when the structure is involved in particulars, it is usually propelled into consideration of policy that should govern in particular situations. When we consider the macropolitical system, we are discussing policy making in its broadest and most synoptic dimensions.

Third, action at this level will be highly political. The devices for submerging politics in administration—prescription of rules and roles, and delegation to professionals—are least effective at this level. Here the issues are open; actors are free to push for de novo consideration of their interests, and they are limited only by the very loose rules of politics; and responses of government are made in terms of the American consensus and the rival powers of contending interests. New unities of purpose to guide subsystem actors may evolve from the process.

The democratic morality cannot be attained unless the central instruments of macropolitics are both representative and effective. Let us look first at the representativeness of these institutions. Party, Congress, and President are the instruments of representation.

The Parties

In the United States the primary function of the parties is to man the government. For Congress, this is effected in two stages. There is the electoral process which produces the membership of the houses. There is thereafter the organizing process in the houses of Congress—the selection of leaders by the members of each party in each house. The majority party gets the most highly strategic positions, but the minority party has in every case parallel positions through which it has opportunities for affirmative as well as negative influence. For President, the choice is by the electorate, from the candidates proposed by the parties.

By organizing a system for selection of leaders the parties make possible the participation in government of the great body of the electorate. It is difficult to conceive of millions of voters having any opportunity to influence the manning of the government without the parties as instruments for recruiting candidates and presenting them as options to the voters.

Given the parties and the electoral process, the macropolitical system is in a broad and loose sense democratic. There are no officials within it that do not directly or indirectly trace their positions back to the people. On the other hand, the degree of attainment of democratic ideals is affected by many factors. I can refer to these only selectively and in large categories.

First, as means of manning the government the electoral processes through which the people select members of Congress and the President do not completely—though they do quite substantially—meet the democratic ideal. Electorates are, of course, given only limited options. Moreover, the selection of candidates offered as options may be greatly influenced by elites—office holders, party workers, party influentials. On the other hand, the conventions and primaries through which nominations are made give extensive opportunities for widely distributed influences. In the case of Congress, nominations are normally made in a primary election; in the case of the President, primaries, public discussion, and the need for getting a candidate that can win popular approval disperse the influences on selection of candidates. The elections themselves meet the standards of an open and free society. The limitations on the suffrage and the distortions against urban representations are being eliminated. Those that exist in the counting of electoral votes for the President may have reduced effects as the sectional differences in the nation are reduced through industrialization, urbanization, and the spread of minority races across the nation. This nation has moved steadily throughout its history toward democratization of the electoral process, and the chief limitation on the representativeness of its government in the future will be the nonparticipation of many to whom rights of participation are offered.

Second, there is some tendency toward the dilution of representation of the poor in the manning of the government. Those who attain positions of power are parts of the upper and middle classes and they have affiliations with power elites. The poor infrequently, if ever, sit in the councils of the mighty.

Third, as means of determining the policies of government, parties and the electoral process break down. There is on policy issues a great vacuum in the guidance of leaders through the electoral process. Platforms do not determine the agenda of government, and if they did, the will of the electorate on each of the issues would not be clear. Issues are blurred in the search of candidates for majority support. Party cohesiveness on issues does not exist in the Congress. The voice of the electorate is not expressed on issues and the will of the nation is placed in commission to the leaders of the government. This is not to say that directions of movement are uninfluenced by elections. The elections of Jefferson, Jackson, Lincoln, McKinley, Wilson, Roosevelt, and Johnson made a difference. But the difference was more in general direction and in personal leadership than in the determination of specific issues in the election.

Fourth, the consequences of the methods of selection of party leaders, and of the weakness of party leadership, in the Congress are of tremendous significance to the democratic character of the macropolitical system. Inherent in them are factors that inhibit attainment of the democratic morality.

The Congress

Leadership in Congress is widely dispersed. It includes, of course, the Speaker, the majority and minority leaders, and others associated with them in the general management of the business of the houses. But it includes also the chairmen and ranking members of the committees.

There is, moreover, a mixing of macropolitical with other functions. Leaders must play the micropolitical game, and indeed leadership positions enhance their ability to play successfully for the selective benefit of their constituents. Macropolitical leadership is also mixed with subsystem activity. The chairman of a committee, excepting the Rules Committee, is deeply immersed in subsystem activity and gains a leadership position by virtue of that activity. Some, of course, move more definitely than others into a position of over-all responsibility. This is true particularly of the chairmen of the appropriations committees. But all leaders except the Speaker, the Minority Floor Leader of the House, and some members of the House Rules Committee, serve on committees with specialized functions.[2] Even the majority and minority leaders of the Senate sit in meetings of committees and subcommittees that deal with specialized program areas.

In sum, the function of top leadership is not fully differentiated. The leader does not get rid of other responsibilities but retains loyalties to constituents and to specialized program demands.

The responsiveness of the leadership to the diverse interests of the nation is distorted by a number of factors. For one thing, the personal stakes of the congressman and his role of local representation may conflict with the leadership role inherent in the position he occupies. As a committee chairman he is entrusted with the double role of compromising conflicting interests within the nation and of searching for national consensus. This national role may be supported by his personal stakes in his party's victory in the nation and in maintaining the favor of a President who is of his party. But he will also have a personal stake in support of combinations of interests that prevail in his constituency.

In addition, the allocation of leadership posts in committees by the seniority rule tends to give position to those who come from districts least affected by the contests of interest on the national stage. The safe seat is the route to committee leadership. The safe seat may give a man the opportunity to rise to a position of statesmanship where he can think in terms of national interests. The chairmen of the Armed Services committees, for example, may be conscious of the fact that their constituents will not react strongly to what they do in this capacity. On the other hand, the safe seat may

2. In 1967 three members of the Rules Committee were members of important joint committees.

provide a chairman an opportunity to obstruct national trends in favor of any sectional views he may represent. Moreover, his committee position has often been selected by a congressman because the committee could affect favorably the interests in his district. This may narrow the perspectives of a committee and of the chairman who heads it. The committees on agriculture, for example, can be expected to overrepresent the interests of agriculture because rural and not urban members of Congress have opted for service on the committee; the chairman almost certainly will be from a district with a high quantity of agricultural interests.

The occupants of leadership positions never have to submit their stewardship to the electorate of the nation. They may be forced toward response to the diversified interests of the nation in a number of ways: by their sharing of the national consensus, their reactions to expert judgment and to other members of Congress and the President, their concern with party victory, and their inescapable participation in compromising interests. On the other hand committees, or committee leaders, may bottle up a piece of legislation and prevent or delay its consideration, and amend legislation or appropriation acts, because of personal stakes identified with narrow constituencies.

If we look at the operation of the Congress in perspective we can see that it has provided a mechanism through which the diverse interests of the nation have been reconciled with sufficient satisfaction to prevent more than minor adjustments in the system since the revolution in the House of Representatives in 1910. This stability could not have been achieved without much responsiveness to the diversified interests of the nation. On the other hand, leadership is distracted to some extent from its national task and is often centered in pockets of narrow responsiveness. The democracy of the process is limited by the qualitative character of the strategic positions that are reconciled through internal bargaining. The manning of congressional positions of leadership, and the rival loyalties created by personal stakes, qualify democratic performance in official roles.

The President

Is the Presidency a truer reflection of democratic ideals? There are factors that support an affirmative answer. First, our constitutional system makes the President the only officer whose sole responsibility is to represent the interests of the nation. Second, he is elected by vote of the people of the whole nation. Third, he occupies the only position in government in which there is enough power to respond effectively to discontent and demand for change in the directions of public policy. Fourth, that position is one of high visibility on which influence can be focused with great effect. The Presidency for these reasons is the main possibility for check upon the autonomy of the administrative state and for initiation of new programs demanded by the dominant interests of the nation.

There are some limitations on the accurate reflection of democratic ideals in this high office. We have noted that power elites have influence on nomination of candidates and that there are distortions in recording and counting the ballot of the people. Specifically, these mechanical distortions include allocation of electoral votes on the basis of representation in Congress—rather than on the number of votes cast in a state—and the counting of the electoral vote of each state as a unit. The effect could be the defeat of a candidate with a majority of the popular vote. History has proved this to be unlikely; the more usual consequence is considerable concentration of the attention of the candidates on the voter blocs that can swing elections in large states. In addition to these effects of the electoral system, the aggregations of influence achieved through organization and group action may have both negative and positive effects on what can be achieved through even the most powerful official in the society. Indeed, minority power blocks—such as those representing tightly organized labor interests or a community of interest in industrial complexes—may have a virtual veto, except in the most unusual circumstances, on the initiatives of the President.

Nevertheless, the nation does have in the Presidency an office that reflects in high degree democratic morality. While the successful candidate may to an extent concentrate his appeal on blocs of votes strategically located, he nevertheless makes a broad appeal to all voters and to all the interests that seek expression in the politics of the nation. His election therefore represents the highest apex of democratic achievement, for it reflects the brokerage of the interests of the nation in an arena of popular discussion and independent expression of popular choice. Moreover, his behavior in office will conform in high measure with the ideal represented in his official role as representative of the nation. While this representation is accomplished by distribution of public benefits among different interests, he is forced by his position to consider the demands and effects of policy upon all the interests of the nation. While he has loyalties to party and to interests that supported his election, he cannot bow to these without considering the reactions in the great national constituency composed of many and varied interests.

His official rectitude—that is, his consideration of all foreseeable effects of his proposals and of his actions—is enforced by the brightest spotlight of diversified publicity ever focused on a public office. He has, indeed, as President Theodore Roosevelt said, a "bully pulpit" from which he can influence public opinion, and he has some ability to cover up relevant facts; but he uses these in an arena of inquiry, criticism, and attack that is open, aggressively searching, and continuous. In addition, presidents have become increasingly conscious of the historical verdict on their stewardship; this appraisal in the future induces care in the assessment of present effects and greater attention to the interests of the new colonials—those having interests tomorrow affected by those who rule today.

The President has, moreover, in recent decades become an active instrument for partial correction of the weighting of influence in favor of the rich and privileged. He has reacted to the interests of the "forgotten man." He has in substantial degree measured up to the hope of Gouverneur Morris in the constitutional convention of 1787 that he would "be the guardian of the people, even of the lower classes."

The President's personal stakes—his own re-election, or election of a successor from his party, and the favorable verdict of history—do accord substantially with the official role he is assigned in our political system. There is much truth in Neustadt's statement, "What is good for the country is good for the President, and *vice versa.*" [3] The representation of the people requires a strong President; the danger is less in the nonrepresentativeness of the Presidency than in the inability of the occupant to perform its tasks.

The Solar System

Senator John F. Kennedy once referred to the total representation of the people in the state legislatures, the two houses of Congress, and the Presidency as the solar system. [4] The imbalances in representation in one arena may be corrected in another. Looking over the span of history we can see many factors that have made the major components of the system more democratic. It may be hoped, and indeed expected, that in the future they will become even more democratic. Some corrections may be made in the electoral

3. Richard E. Neustadt, *Presidential Power: The Politics of Leadership* (New York: John Wiley & Sons, Inc., 1960), p. 185.
4. In Senate debates in 1956 on reform of the electoral college. See the summary in *Congress and the Nation, 1945–1964: A Review of Government and Politics in the Postwar Years* (Washington, D.C.: Congressional Quarterly Service, 1965), p. 1523.

college system; "one man, one vote" decisions will in time correct an element of misrepresentation in the Congress; and the effects of pockets of narrow responsiveness in Congress may be reduced by presidential leadership, by amendment of the rules of the two houses of Congress, and by increasing uniformity in economic and social conditions in the nation and an accompanying homogenization of politics that will reduce the effects of sectional blocs and safe seats.

THE EFFECTIVENESS OF MACROPOLITICAL CONTROLS

The themes of this section are that macropolitical functions are heavily concentrated in the Presidency as an institution and that they overload the President personally.

Because of its size, bicameral structure, diversity, and the weakness of nationally oriented leadership, Congress is unable to participate effectively in many of the macropolitical functions. Crisis decisions require unity and dispatch, co-ordinative decisions require unity. Some co-ordination is achieved through new legislative rules for the administrative state and the appropriation process, but beyond these things co-ordination, like crisis decisions, will be achieved primarily in the executive branch. Congress is weak also on decisions on persons to man the government. When exercised with respect to rank and file, particularly local officials, congressional participation degenerates into micropolitics; and for major officials, the authority of the Senate is seldom negatively employed against an executive recommendation—though, of course, individuals in Congress may influence executive appointments.

While crisis and co-ordinative functions are peculiarly executive by virtue of their requirements, the responsibility of defining programs and rules and roles, allocating resources, and reviewing operations are shared more fully by the two branches and the President. Respecting the first two of these, initiative and leadership have passed to a substantial extent to the President. His legislative recommendations, his budget, the priorities he sets among proposals in both, and the selective pressures exerted by him with respect to these substantially determine the agenda of Congress and its committees. Nevertheless, Congress has survived as a hardy instrument of legislation and budgeting. Initiatives in congressional committees still elevate issues of lawmaking and budgeting into macropolitics, laws are still framed in Congress as they were in the days of great congressional leaders like Sam Rayburn and Robert Wagner, amendments change the content of executive proposals, and negatives on such proposals are freely imposed. On legislation and appropriations, there is vitality in both the President and Congress.

The review function of Congress appears to be even hardier. There are hazards in it that have frightened those who wanted strength in administrative agencies: micropolitical intervention, strength of the high-quantity interests that find representation in congressional segments of subsystems, and harassment of agencies and impairment of their effectiveness by detailed supervision. There are hazards also in dissipation of the energies of congressmen and their staffs. The review function is exercised intermittently, fragmentally, and with such discordant voices that its effects are often inconclusive. Its most effective exercise is in the appropriations subcommittees where expansions and contractions of programs are effected. In spite of its deficiencies, the review function of Congress is part of the citizen's access to the administrative state and another line of protection against the possibilities that the latter will not be sufficiently open to affected interests.

Another set of centers for the exercise of macropolitical controls is the departmental offices of the executive branch. These share the functions of the President as portrayed in the blue- and green-line systems on Chart II in Chapter III. Secretary McNamara has shown the potentialities of aggressive departmental leadership and he left behind him instruments of departmental co-ordination and control that may weaken permanently the independence of the operating units within the Department of Defense. Nevertheless such departmental leadership and the opportunities for it are rare, and the deposit of strength in the departmental leadership will still be impaired by activities of separate services, congressional committees, and interest groups. Departmental chieftains normally preside over an aggregation of quasi-independent agencies or bureaus and find it difficult to resist their separatistic urges and self-promotional activities.

Chart IV presents an outline of the major roles of the departmental overhead in the Department of Agriculture—a typical aggregation of separate agencies—together with a summary of specific functions to be performed. In scope these latter are quite extensive, but effectiveness in their exercise is limited by several factors. First, there is substantial independence in the agencies. They have knowledge that is difficult, if not impossible, to match at the departmental level. They are defensive of traditional ways of doing things. They have strong subsystem connections with clienteles and congressional committees. They are manned by civil service employees—even the heads of the agencies are sometimes civil service employees. This, for example, is the status of the head of the Forest Service. In addition, the chief of the service and all of his principal assistants will usually have been promoted from the rank of forester, which is the entry grade into the Forest Service. Even one of the assistant secretaries of the department—that for administration—legally now has civil service status. Second, the secretary has difficulty in recruiting a staff of the size, knowledge, and skills, and with the tenure on the job, required to penetrate the complexities of policy making and administration in the agencies. Finally, the secretary lacks a clientele of his own to which he can appeal in any instance in which his views are not fully shared by the agencies. He has to depend on his own dynamism and skill, the competence of a small group of associates, and the

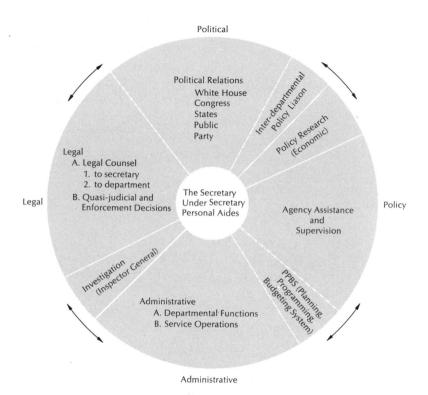

Chart IV Departmental Functions

Functions To Be Performed at the Departmental Level

1. Transmit political purpose.
   Current examples: civil rights, cost saving, rural poverty, PPBS.
2. Provide political protection and support—for the President, the department, and agencies.
3. Obtain rule adherence and procedural formulation.
   In such areas as personnel, accounting, budget processes, and usually in a channel from the Civil Service Commission, General Accounting Office, General Services Administration, and the Bureau of the Budget to the agencies.
4. Co-ordinate and stimulate program development.
   As convenor for group discussions, by settlement of conflicts, by clearances, and by policy directives.
5. Regulate the scale of program and administrative growth.
   Positively: initiating new programs, supporting agency programs.
   Negatively: by restraints ranging from veto to weak support or reference to a restraining center outside the department.

support of the President. His power position is weak unless he taps that of the President, and this recourse is of limited utility to him because it has to be distributed in so many directions.

The focus of the macropolitical system, as we have noted, is the Presidency. The capabilities of the system for giving direction to the administrative state is heavily dependent upon the capacity of the Presidency and its occupant. That capacity, and the limits upon it, are both institutional and personal. The capacities of the Presidency have been enormously expanded by institutional development of the office. The effect of this development is to create a continuing set of macroadministrative institutions and processes to deal with the top-level functions of government which are inherently, or which at any moment may become, matters of general public concern. The President, at the top of the macropolitical structure, has the assistance of macroadministrative institutions.

The structure of the macroadministrative institutions has on the whole evolved recently. An early element in the structure was the Civil Service Commission, but it was long an instrument of restraint on political influence rather than of positive direction of government. Today it can be given an official role in implementing a policy; for example, the President has delegated to it the role of framing the rules and policing the departments and agencies of government to prevent discrimination in employment in the civil service. The next entry was the Bureau of the Budget, which extends the reach of the Presidency into budgeting and managerial aspects of administration. It has served also as a center for co-ordination of the tremendously effective processes, developed largely under Presidents Truman and Eisenhower, for formulating the President's legislative program, which emerges in the State of the Union message and a succeeding flow of legislative proposals by special message. Since World War II other institutions have been added: the Council of Economic Advisers, the National Security Council and affiliated organizations, the Office of Emergency Planning, and the Office of Science and Technology. Also, the President has had since 1939 the benefit of a White House staff that can offer personal aid and give assistance on functions that have not been institutionalized in executive office organizations.

The evolution of *macroadministrative institutions* and the accompanying linkage of departmental structures with them is assuredly not completed. We may see its amplification in such areas as natural resources, social welfare, and economic policy, in all of which there is a wide scattering of policy making and administrative roles in the executive branch.

While macroadministration can expand the reach of the Presidency, it cannot eliminate the burden on the President himself. He must make decisions on legislative proposals, allocation of resources, and staffing the government. Moreover, there is an increasing number of crisis decisions in both international and domestic affairs which demand the personal attention of the President, in part because no lesser official can be entrusted with them, in part because no lesser official has the power to make a decision stand. This is true in domestic as well as international crises—only the President, for example, has the power to stand up against the barons of industry and labor when the activities of either threaten inflation or the stoppage of essential industry.

It has already been noted, however, that the President cannot involve himself in all the problems that are of concern to the people of the American nation. He, like the instruments of Congress, can give attention only intermittently and selectively to most of the problems of the nation. He must, moreover, carefully husband his political influence for the interventions that require his official and personal prestige. He has to gain support in the wide arena of popular reaction for what he proposes to do. Moreover, much of what he does requires the collaboration of the leaders in the seats of power in Congress, and hence the selective expenditure of his influence to achieve this collaboration and the support of other congressmen.

These things must be of deep concern to those who are subjects in the administered society. In crisis situations—such as Berlin, Cuba, the Dominican Republic, and Vietnam —where decisions are irrevocable, or revocable with difficulty, and affect profoundly our lives, we have to be concerned more with the possibilities of mistakes than with the power of the office of President. In these situations our fate must be entrusted to a person with power; we must hope that his vision will be wide, his information true and adequate, and his choices made with correct appraisal of consequences. But there are other limitations on the Presidency that will be of concern to us. The Bay of Pigs incident in 1961 and public revelations of the Central Intelligence Agency's activities in 1966 show the danger that the President can be trapped or the nation unprotected by the independence of administrative units from adequate overhead control. And there are myriad issues of public policy that are kicked around in committees of Congress and in public discussion without political power ever being assembled for constructive action.

Neither the strength nor the spread of attention of the President will be equal to the role imposed on him. Time is not available today or tomorrow. In the face of the fickleness of public opinion toward the President, the independence of strategic positions in Congress, and the power of organized interests in the nation, a President must choose times and subjects for intervention. Every President must have looked regretfully at things that he would have liked to do but could not. The President too, along with the rest of us, is a prisoner of the political-administrative system.

CONCLUSIONS

The most important decisions for the public sector of the administered society must be made in the macropolitical institutions. To serve the democratic morality, these institutions must be both representative and effective. In certain general respects the institutions are demonstrably representative: the President and members of Congress are selected in open and free elections; the two together provide the multiple access that is necessary for representation of interests in a pluralistic society; they have reconciled the diverse and often conflicting interests sufficiently to gain general acceptance from diverse interests in the society they serve. In some specific respects the institutions fall short of the democratic ideal: interest groups of various types gain disproportionate influence in the electoral process and in policy decisions; in composition and associations the people's representatives are largely upper middle class; and the manning and independence of congressional leadership positions unbalances the representation of interests. Yet the nation has moved progressively toward more representative institutions, and this tendency may be expected to continue.

Democratic representation of the interests of the people may be lost through ineffectiveness of the instruments of overhead democracy. The dangers are that too much may be done in administrative institutions without the attention of the overhead leadership, and that too few of the interests that can be served best by new programs or by changes in rules and roles will gain attention from the representatives of the people.

For these problems of representation and effectiveness three kinds of solution deserve attention. First, the effectiveness of macropolitical institutions depends upon the organization of macroadministrative institutions and processes. Both Congress and the President can be effective only if roles of planning, policy development, and continuing review exist. Complex government calls for big administration represented in continuing roles of actors at the top level of government. Part of the answer of democratic government for the administrative state is bigger administration; that is to say, the Bureau of the Budget, the Council of Economic Advisers, and other institutional arrangements for macroadministration supply part of the answer for democratic government.

Second, the ideal of democratic government calls for the major public issues to be placed on the agenda of government for consideration. There have been many proposals looking toward more effective co-operation between the President and Congress, such as four-year terms for members of the House of Representatives, joint executive-legislative councils, and even the election of some members of Congress on a national ticket. I submit that the basic problem lies in the pockets of narrow responsiveness in the leadership posts of Congress. Congressional revision of rules on discharge of committees or on methods of appointment of chairmen are the types of solution most often proposed. Parliamentary governments have another solution: the legislature sets aside time for consideration of Cabinet proposals. While the parliamentary system is alien to our institutions and traditions, Congress could allow some of its time for debate and floor consideration of whatever measures the President may submit for priority consideration, in whatever form he may wish to propose them. The ability of leaders, unanswerable to the nation as a whole, to block consideration of measures of legislation is out of accord both with the trend toward presidential leadership in legislation and with the ideals of democratic government. *By some technique* this unrepresentative element of our system needs to be eliminated or restricted, if the system is to be made more democratic.

Third, the review function can probably not be adequately exercised by one branch of government alone. The independence, the opportunities for secrecy, and the traditionalism of administrative agencies, together with the possibilities for ignoring or overlooking new interests pressing for consideration within the bureaucracy, call for some kind (or kinds) of ombudsman. The methods of Congress in exercising the review function are not perfect and have not had adequate consideration, but it is not likely that the function will be adequately performed without congressional participation in it.

VI

Man as Subject of Administration

THE LAST FOUR CHAPTERS have treated broadly and generally the representation of interests through the policies and operations of the administrative state. They have treated administration in terms of programs, institutions, and rules and roles that represent concurrent interests, mediate interests, and reflect choices among interests. Administration has been viewed as part of a political process through which benefits are allocated to groups and persons.

As a result of the process more and more interests are served by the activities of the administrative state. In health, education, welfare, fire and police protection, services to business groups, and innumerable other areas, men's interests are served so largely by the continuing activity of specialized administrative institutions that it would be impossible to visualize life without these services. We can view the administrative state as the servant of interests that have prevailed in the total process resulting in the creation and continued operation of specialized agencies. Administration is, in this view, the unfolding and allocation of the services of the state. Ultimately, however, man stands on the receiving line where he is more subject than participant with respect to these services. He finds he is the recipient of the services, or of disadvantages resulting from their being rendered to others. He is the subject of administration. The administrative state is there and he must come to terms with it.

To a large extent the services of administration are accepted without active objection to either the services or the way they are performed; otherwise the feelings of deprivation of liberty would strain the consensus or acquiescence on which successful administration depends. Even as service to some results in constraints upon others—as is generally true, either through regulations or denials, or imposition of taxes —the subjects of such constraint accept them. In a society where protest is as easy as in ours, and where many people regard it as part of their liberty to violate a law they do not believe in, and where all regard it as part of their liberty to seek changes in law and its administration, the continuity of administrative services and controls strongly indicates widespread participation through voluntary, instead of coerced, acceptance. Acceptance may be, however, the result of acquiescence because of subordinate position, lack of information about means of petition or protest that are open, or unavailability of effective channels for citizen action against administration.

Dissatisfied people do sometimes demand abolition of this or that activity of administration, as is illustrated by the abandonment of Prohibition, the prompt dissolution of wartime controls in 1945–47, and the protests against the war in Vietnam. Also, dissatisfied people may seek new balances in administration, as is exemplified in the passage of the Taft-Hartley Act in 1947. The political processes described in earlier chapters supply means for response to such discontents. They also supply the means for discussion of much smaller adjustments in policy and administration. Yet men will be subject to administration in its continuous aspects. In this chapter we will look at some of the problems presented by this subjection of man to power.

THE SPIRIT OF ADMINISTRATION

The basic requirement of democratic morality is that people be treated humanely. This means treatment of each person with respect for him as an individual and with due consideration of his rights, interests, and feelings. Some men face the power of the administrative state with arrogance or rebellion; others with fear, distrust, or discomfort; others still with complete equanimity. All deserve respectful consideration of legitimate inquiries and complaints.

In a democratic society leaders will be under some compulsion to seek attainment of program objectives with the minimum of restraint, deprivation, and punitiveness. The spirit of such a society is antagonistic to unnecessary constraint or encumbrance upon individuals. Moreover, the leaders in such a society are conscious of the freedom of dissent and criticism, and of the ability of persons to gain sympathy and to marshal effective support against harsh administration. These things are reflected in our administrative practice. Laws often provide sanctions which are weak, and when the legal sanctions are severe administrators seek softer means of gaining compliance. Indeed, they usually strive for understanding of their objectives as the primary means of obtaining general, voluntary compliance. There is indeed a danger, well known to administrators, that the constraints toward leniency will impair the ability of administration to maintain the integrity of program objectives.

Yet there are other dangers. Administrators may be apathetic toward human rights and feelings, or neglectful of attention to these. There is danger also of a kind of two-worldism in which some individuals are dealt with attentively and others with condescension, harshness, or unconcern. There may be a mild answer or even capitulation to the influential, but a firm *no* to the man who lacks influence. The double standard does not exist in the moral code alone!

It is difficult to gauge the spirit of the administrative state in its many variations. We can note the gentle approach of the traffic officer to the law violator, or the restraint of the police in handling a riot, or we can note the turning of police dogs on minority people in the streets of Birmingham. To get a truer gauge we may have to leave the sunlight of the streets and sit overnight in a municipal police station, visit a jail or an institution for the mentally ill, observe the handling of problem children in a school principal's office, look at the treatment of a relief client, observe the questioning of an alleged communist, sit in the forums where the rights of conscientious objectors are determined, or contemplate the severity or lack of severity in sentences imposed on those adjudged guilty of the most offensive crimes.

The policy of the law and the sentiments of the people have sometimes called for harsh treatment of individuals by administrative agents. We can note the treatment of our Japanese residents and of conscientious objectors in World War II,[1] the sweep of McCarthyism after the war, and the inattention to the rights of Negroes and the poor in distressed condition or when charged with law violation. But traditional antibureaucratic and libertarian sentiments among our people, the wide spread of humanitarian and nonauthoritarian ideals, and the means of protest existing in society, have long tempered administrative practice in this country. The trends in policy and administrative practice are now definitely in the direction of empathy for men of every group. This is no doubt due both to the stirring of the democratic conscience and to the response of government to the participation of minorities. Whatever the causes, we can see reflections of a new humaneness in the relations of policy and administration to people.

1. See Alexander Leighton, *The Governing of Men* (Princeton, N.J.: Princeton University Press, 1945), and Mulford Q. Sibley and Philip E. Jacob, *Conscription of Conscience: The American State and the Conscientious Objector, 1940–1947* (Ithaca, N.Y.: Cornell University Press, 1952).

THE ELEMENTS OF PROTECTION
FOR SUBJECTS OF ADMINISTRATION

The subjection of man to administration is not new, and we can find in our traditional administrative law four primary principles for protection of the citizen before administration. They are notice, opportunity to be heard, decision without bias, and independent review. These four rudimentary principles of justice, asserted in some old areas of administration, supply the standards for a modern charter of constitutionalism in the relations of citizens to the powerful and pervasive modern administrative state. They cannot be implemented by law alone, and they do not meet all the needs for protection of the citizen. They cannot take the place of correction through political process, or of effective administrative organization and internal decisional processes. But they are essential for protection of the rights of men before administration and for embodiment of the democratic ideal in administrative practice. They are guides for nonlegal (informal) as well as legal (formal) administrative practice.

Notice—The Right To Know

The fundamental principle of notice is that man has a right to be alerted to activity that affects his interests. It asserts the right of the person to know the action that may be taken. In the administrative law governing property taxation, for example, it is the rule that a man has a right to be informed of any increase in his individual tax assessment. The notice that is required in administrative cases is normally personal; but when the location of the party cannot be known or many persons are affected, notice by publication is the necessary substitute. There are exceptions to the rule requiring notice, but the rule has wide application in administrative law. Today it is being expanded in the administrative law relating to the administration of justice: the police are now under certain obligations to inform an arrested person of his rights, including his right to remain silent or to consult with counsel.[2]

The principle of notice has been expanded and implemented through legislation. The judicial requirement of notice has not usually been applied to rule-making proceedings. Statute has, however, expanded the requirement. In addition to special statutory requirements for particular situations, the Administrative Procedure Act requires, with exceptions, notice of proposed rule making in the Federal Register.[3]

Legal rules of these kinds, while basic, do not provide the notice that is required for democratic practice. They will not, by themselves, even be sufficient for the professional whose business it is to help people understand their rights in administration. The gap between these formal requirements and the need of people for information is very wide. The means of filling the gap differ in different programs, but there are four general ways by which it is filled.

One is by administrative arrangements for publicity and individual notice. When medicare was instituted for example, general publicity in the press was supplemented by distribution through the post offices of information to the aged. Agencies with established programs affecting large numbers of people, such as the Social Security Administration, put out millions of folders that provide affected persons with clear and simple descriptions of program benefits. They also try to obtain the attention of the press for notable changes in their programs. But seldom is the precise information needed by a citizen about a program affecting his welfare obtainable from the general press alone.

The second means is private distribution of information to affected groups. The publishing houses that assemble and distribute legal materials and indexes of these perform this service for lawyers, accountants, and others who must have

2. Escobedo v. Illinois, 378 U.S. 478 (1964).
3. 60 Stat. 237 (1946), Section 4(a).

complete data in order to serve their clients effectively. Trade associations are now the chief channel for keeping business and occupational groups informed of their rights and liabilities. I recall that the restaurant association in a southwestern state increased its membership tenfold during World War II as a result of the need of restaurant owners for information on price, wage, rationing, and manpower regulations. Today the largest business firms support their own facilities for obtaining information, but business and occupational groups will normally get the information they need through trade associations. Group activity is an important means of informing people of the effects of administration on their interests.

The third means is through field contacts of administrators with citizens. The Social Security Administration, for example, has field offices all over the country from which citizens can obtain information by telephone or personal visit; it arranges also for staff members of these offices to be on duty in outlying cities and communities on certain days of the week. Even compliance checks—e.g. bank inspections, or checks by agents of the Wage and Hour and Public Contracts divisions—can be means of informing persons of the precise requirements to which they are subject.

The final means is through independent study of the informal processes of administration and resultant publication. This may be means of informing professionals so that they can give better service to their clients; for example, the lawyer who has had an opportunity to learn through his own experience or the study and publication of others the ways in which the Food and Drug Administration and the Federal Trade Commission operate may be better able as a result to give legal aid on matters affecting branding and advertising of products. It is, in addition, a means of informing the elites whose continuous surveillance of administration is necessary to keep it responsive to the ideals of society.

Difficulties are encountered frequently by those who try to perform this function of penetrating the administrative

veil that hides informal processes. Information is incomplete
and is scattered in a labyrinth of files; documents are marked
"restricted" for protection of administrative secrecy (rather
than national security); officials are reluctant to reveal inner
processes; they are fearful also that they, other persons, or
the agency will suffer if policy controversies are uncovered;
and it is difficult to obtain access to the chief participants in
policy making. Yet the degree of openness of administration
to observation, study, and criticism is much greater than in
most countries. Organizations like the Inter-University Case
Committee have been able to gain access for studies inside
administrative organizations that provide intimate pictures
of internal processes.

We cannot accept the idea that the citizen must depend
upon self-help to learn what the government is doing and
how it affects him. In a democratic society each agency must
bear a responsibility for informing people of the benefits and
liabilities of its program and, except as required for national
security or the privacy of its staff, for making its processes
known to society. It may be possible some day to put most of
the kinds of questions that people would ask about administrative services and controls in a single data bank, from which
officers in field stations could provide the information re-
quested by citizens. But it will still be necessary to give
specific notice to particular persons and groups whose interests are affected by administration.

The Opportunity To Be Heard—
The Right to Access

Administrative law asserted the principle that a man had a
right to be heard at some point in process before his rights
were finally determined. In property tax law, for example, a
person had a right to a hearing before some forum before
his individual tax assessment was finally fixed.[4] This is a

4. See for illustration Hagar v. Reclamation District, 111 U.S. 701 (1884), and
Nickey v. Mississippi, 292 U.S. 393, 396 (1934).

specific formulation of what in modern terminology we refer to in broader terms as the right to access. The opportunity for a hearing makes effective and meaningful the right of access to the decisional authority that allocates benefits and disadvantages to persons.

The right of a hearing and to what is regarded as an appropriate kind of hearing is now embodied in many statutes and for affairs administered in national administration is stated in a comprehensive statute—the Administrative Procedure Act of 1946. It defines the procedural rights of persons in what are known as adjudicatory proceedings. It goes a step further. It assumes that, when the policy-making (rule making) process is carried from legislative to administrative forums, those affected by administrative rules should have, with stated exceptions, the right to present in oral or written form their views on proposed rules.

This statute gets so much attention in repeated hearings of Congress and in the discussions of the bar that there is danger that the important principle it embodies will be considered in too narrow a framework. Effective access to the agencies of the administrative state in matters affecting one's interests requires much more than can be embodied in a procedural statute.

There is, first, the problem of cost. I noted earlier that Dean Landis stated that the expenses of administrative procedure were so large as to make it unavailable to many.[5] To meet this problem administrative agencies have had to struggle, often against the opposition of the organized bar, both to simplify formal procedures and, more importantly, to construct informal procedures through which consideration could be given to men's interests under administration. To most men, for example, the aid of local internal revenue offices in preparing their income tax returns and competent and considerate attention to controversial issues by the ad-

5. *Supra,* p. 95.

ministrative staffs in these offices is more important than the opportunity for formal hearings and appeals. In addition, in the most vital of all proceedings affecting a person—those in which he is accused of a felony—the Supreme Court has now held that the state must provide for the defense of the indigent accused.[6] Effective representation of the interests of persons may require extension of this principle to misdemeanors and to some types of civil proceedings.[7]

Second, access of the individual to administration, as to the legislatures through which it is directed, may often be dependent upon effective group activity. I need only note the activities of trade associations, labor unions, the National Association for the Advancement of Colored People, and the American Civil Liberties Union, to indicate how the access of men, and a hearing for their interests, may be achieved by organizations which supply representation for them.

Third, access on behalf of the individual may be provided by the positive roles of administrative agencies, for roles may be created for administrators which provide for the individual access he cannot achieve by self-help alone. To illustrate, the interests of consumers are represented through the action of cities against public utilities, the appearances of government agencies before rate-making bodies, the laboratory testing of products by government purchasing agents, the inspection of premises, and the activities of the Food and Drug Administration. The right to vote was pushed forward in the South by the role of the Civil Rights Division of the Department of Justice in implementing the registration provisions of the Civil Rights Act of 1964. In the giant administrative state, citizen interests before administration can often be achieved

6. Gideon v. Wainwright, 372 U.S. 335 (1963).
7. While the Supreme Court of the United States has denied certiorari to review decisions denying counsel in misdemeanor cases (Winters v. Beck, 385 U.S. 907 [1966] and DeJoseph v. Connecticut, 385 U.S. 982 [1966]), the Supreme Court of Minnesota (State v. Borst, 154 N.W. 888 [1967]) and the Court of Appeals of Alabama (Irvin v. State, 8 Div. 111 [1967]) have upheld the right to appointed counsel in a minor offense where jail is a possibility.

only if strategic positions have been created in administration through which influence can be exerted upon other positions. This lateral administrative activity provides a means of continuous hearing for personal and group interests.

Finally, the opportunity to be heard is often dependent upon special administrative arrangements by which individual inquiries, petitions, and complaints can be pressed. For example, field offices may provide the only facility through which a person can get an opportunity to present his claims. The Bureau of Prisons' steps to protect a prisoner's right of access is peculiarly illustrative of the point. It has given prisoners the right to send uncensored and unopened letters to public agencies, the courts, and members of the House and Senate.

In sum, the right of access is secured, often most effectively, through means other than personal hearing. The right to be personally heard through formal hearings or in some other way is nevertheless important. This right may be achieved within an organization supplying services or regulating the life of people. It may also be obtained through appeal to other forums, which will be discussed presently.

The Rule against Bias—
The Right to a Fair Forum
Notice and the opportunity to present one's case will be meaningless if the decision or action which follows is made in a forum which is closed or prejudiced against consideration of the interest asserted. The principles of administrative justice assume a fair forum. Traditional administrative law gave a measure of protection to this objective by its standard that one should not participate in deciding on a matter on which he had any personal bias toward one of the parties in a controversy. The framers of the Administrative Procedure Act sought to safeguard the principle in various ways, notably by trying to ensure the independence of the examiners who made or recommended adjudicatory decisions and by trying

to prevent a mixture of prosecutory and judiciary functions in the same persons on the staffs of administrative agencies.[8] Statutes and administrative practice have sought to ensure independence from bias in many ways, including among others the exclusion of appointment to administrative positions of persons having personal stakes and the exclusion of participation of persons in such positions in those administrative decisions in which they have conflicts of interests which would impair fairness in judgment.

Yet no problem, either of justice or of efficiency in the consideration of the interests of the subjects of the administrative state, is any more difficult than this problem of bias in the composition of the forums of administrative decision. What we have said earlier indicates that it is not possible to eliminate biases as to contending interests in the administrative state. Administration is the servant of politics. The victory of those who win in the macropolitical contest is registered in the creation of official roles in administration that embody their interests, and the contest of interests for influence on those roles is continued in macropolitics, subsystem politics, and micropolitics. The choices and mediation among interests is carried over into biases of administrative organizations. The decisions to have a Federal Reserve System in which bankers will have a dominant role, to have regulatory commissions which will mediate interests, to have tripartite boards in labor-management administration to mediate conflicting interests, and to have medical personnel in top administrative posts in health departments, all reflect biases built into the administrative structure toward dominant or influential interests.

Moreover, the use of professionals in administration and the establishment of positions create, as we saw in Chapter II, professional biases and personal-stake biases. If illustration is needed, one can look at the action of a university faculty

8. 60 Stat. 237 (1946), Sections 5 and 11.

on curriculum requirements. When the issues on what courses shall be required are debated, hardly anyone is in a position to think in an unbiased manner about the interest of the student in a good education; his professional biases on what is important and his personal stakes in what is required have rendered him incompetent for unbiased decision.

What then would a workable concept of democracy require of administration with respect to the biases of administrative forums? First, that the political processes through which official biases are determined shall be open to diversified access representative of all persons in the society. Second, that the official roles of organizations and persons in the administrative state determined in the political process shall be dominant, through all the means ingenuity can devise, over rival biases. Third, that in the application of policy to individuals, devices for programming categories of administrative action to prevent discrimination among persons in the same circumstances—such as were discussed in the chapter on micropolitics—shall be consciously sought. And finally, that there shall be appropriate moderation of the bias toward the service objectives of administrative agencies in favor of humane treatment of those who are subjects of administration.

The administrative law on bias rejected the idea that administration should not be biased toward the objective for which it was established. It is appropriate that the judge and the police should be biased against murder when law has proscribed murder, and that the educator, the health official, the draft board, and the administrator in the National Labor Relations Board should be biased in favor of the policies, rules, and official roles prescribed for or inherent in their positions. But the service objectives, and the allegiance of administrative personnel thereto, should be qualified by fair and humane consideration of the interests of persons. This conflict between men as rulers through their institutions and men as subjects is always, as noted in the first chapter, a quandary of democratic theory; the quandary calls for complementary biases—on the one hand toward the effectiveness of the service, on the other toward methods required by the dignity of men subject to the service.[9]

Independent Review—The
Right to Appeal

Administrative law has given to the individual some rights of appeal from administrative decision and action to the courts, thus providing an independent review of administrative activity. Criminal action or civil suits traditionally offered means of confining the administrator's action to the official role set for him by the law. Statutes have piecemeal, though sometimes broadly—as in the Administrative Procedure Act, defined or amplified the rights of direct appeal or collateral attack in the courts. The jurisdiction of the courts traditionally has been the means of monitoring administration to protect the rights of the individual.

That means, although essential, falls far short of what is required for effective independent review on behalf of the subject of administration. Innumerable types of actions by administrators do not come within the rules covering what is justiciable or for practical reasons outside the scope of judicial notice; the costs of appeal to courts is often prohibitive; specific types of activity are often exempted from judicial review; the delays and the limitations on the kinds of remedies the courts can provide restrict the effectiveness of judicial process in individual instances. The remedies of the courts are not adequate for general correction of maladministration; and the courts acting through judicial processes could not carry the burden if the subjects of administration really tried to protect their innumerable interests in fair treatment under administration by this method. Judicial protection has not been adjusted to keep pace with the expansion of the administrative state.

There are two purposes in independent review. One is to get consideration of the individual case, and for this the

9. See Chapter VII for discussion of this reconciliation of objectives in the relations of the worker to the organization in which he serves.

right of personal appeal is crucial. The other is correction of the practice of administration so that causes for complaint will not arise. The courts cannot be expected to be able to meet the second need, and are a sometimes-available, last resort for the first.

The needs are partially met by an equivalence of independent review within the administrative structure itself. Surveys of administrative practice—either by agencies themselves, by specialized agencies such as the Bureau of the Budget and the Comptroller General, or by outside groups —have been common in this country in the twentieth century. Such surveys deal most frequently with agency efficiency, but they sometimes include attention to protective arrangements for individual rights and interests. Agencies may have special continuing arrangements for receiving or uncovering individual complaints, such as procedures for receiving and answering complaints, or inspection or audit units to check upon operating officials. The Bureau of Prisons has been referred to as an example of the first; examples of the second are found in the Field Inspection Unit of the Immigration and Naturalization Service and the Office of the Inspector General in the Department of Agriculture—an office directly responsible to the secretary of the department with the ambitious assignment of seeing that "nowhere in this Department are functions, people, facilities, or programs being used unfairly." [10] Perhaps, however, there is an inevitable tendency in such offices to devote more attention to what is necessary to protect the agency or the government than to what is needed to protect complaining individuals, although it is possible to serve both purposes by the same procedure.

Another means available to the person subject to national administration is appeal to his congressman and senators. This is often a more meaningful means of complaint and redress than appeal to the courts. Congressmen are in an

10. See Walter Gellhorn, *When Americans Complain: Governmental Grievance Procedures* (Cambridge, Mass.: Harvard University Press, 1966), pp. 114–21.

important sense a corps of American ombudsmen. The congressman has ears for his constituents and is willing to be their "legman" and often their special pleader. He regards himself as a humanizer of administration and undoubtedly this view is widely shared among constituents.

This is not a perfect device. It may create more harassment for administration than is justified by the need for external review, it diverts congressmen's attention away from legislative duties, and it often creates micropolitical pressures that impair the fairness and efficiency of administration. Walter Gellhorn has noted other disadvantages: ". . . (a) it too often shortcircuits administrative processes that should be allowed or, if need be, forced to run their course; (b) it too often aims merely at giving a congressman an unearned credit; and (c) it too infrequently includes thought about the future." [11]

The independent review of Congress over administration has another element besides casework for constituents. This is the continuing oversight of administration through the processes of budget consideration and inquiry by standing committees, supplemented by investigations. These activities are not unrelated in the day-to-day affairs of Congress to the kinds of complaints that congressmen receive from constituents, and they are means of giving attention to the general practice of administration and the correction of that practice. With all its imperfections, congressional oversight—achieved through both casework and committee inquiry—is an important means of assuring both a right of appeal and independent reviews of administrative practice.

PROBLEMS FOR CONSIDERATION

To provide further protection to man as subject of administration it is desirable in our day to give consideration to extension of the citizen's remedies on three fronts. First, now

11. Ibid. p. 125.

that we know about the experience with the office of ombudsman in Denmark, Finland, Norway, Sweden, and New Zealand, we need to seek ways of filling gaps in our machinery for receiving and considering complaints. In all of these countries the ombudsman is a prestigious official who, independent of the executive branch, receives complaints of all types; investigates them with the power of unlimited access to official records; communicates his conclusions to complainants, administrative officials, and the public; and, in some places, institutes prosecutions. In all countries, however, communication of recommendations to agencies and pressure for their acceptance in the chief instrument of the ombudsman.[12]

What relevance does this experience abroad have to our national administration? Walter Gellhorn, in a careful treatment of the question, concludes: "A single all-embracing ombudsman in the Scandinavian style might drown in a sea of genuine or fancied grievances before he could even begin to function." [13] He shows also that "Washington's woods are full of external critics of administration." [14] But the imperfections in our present system, in which reliance is placed heavily on the 535 congressional ombudsmen, lead him to suggest three possible lines of advance: First, the Administrative Conference of the United States, authorized as a continuing body by Congress in 1964 but initiated only in January 1968, has an opportunity to become a means of discovery and correction, particularly since the conference has a link with the agencies through their representation therein. Headed by a chairman with independence and a good salary, the conference has the function of inquiring into "matters proposed by persons inside or outside the Federal Government." It will be interesting to observe whether the conference will be adequately supported by appropriations

12. Ibid. pp. 9–10, 45–47.
13. Ibid. p. 128.
14. Ibid. p. 124.

and whether it can weave itself into the areas of administration where the rights and the interests of the ordinary man and the poor of the nation are most intimately affected, or whether it will be a poorly supported agency dealing with the highly technical issues of procedure in areas already the subjects of repeated inquiry.

Second, there is Congressman Henry Reuss's proposal for a central bureau of retail casework to which congressmen could refer inquiries and complaints for investigation and report. The issue here, Gellhorn says, is whether such a center would be "more concerned about having sound judgment applied to constituents' grievances and less concerned about squeezing out of them every last drop of campaign juice." [15] Finally, "the administrative agencies must be constantly encouraged to perfect their own grievance machinery, so that small dissatisfactions can be erased without anyone's having to mount a crusade." [16]

What relevance does foreign experience with the ombudsman have for our state and local administration? Patently much more than for national administration, because of the lack of effective legislative watchmanship in most states and the multitude of state and local functions touching the daily life and interests of the individual. Moreover, the smaller size of these jurisdictions is less inhibitory of general complaint bureaus. The ombudsman experience should be a challenge to every state and city to consider the possibilities of improvement of the protections of the citizen, either by ombudsmen with general jurisdiction over all complaints or by those with jurisdiction over specialized areas of administration where the citizen's rights are most likely to be overlooked.

The second front calling for concentrated attention concerns protection of the privacy of the citizen. The importance of this front has been comprehensively and graphically por-

15. Ibid. p. 129.
16. Ibid.

trayed in Alan F. Westin's recently published *Privacy and Freedom*.[17] Westin begins with a definition: "Privacy is the claim of individuals, groups, or institutions to determine for themselves when, how, and to what extent information about them is communicated to others." [18] He finds that virtually all animals and men in all stages of history have had need for periods of individual seclusion or small-group intimacy,[19] but that there is also a universal "tendency on the part of individuals to invade the privacy of others, and of society to engage in surveillance to guard against anti-social conduct." [20] In the United States we have "an egalitarian democratic balance, in which the privacy-supporting values of individualism, associational life, and civil liberty are under constant pressure from privacy-denying tendencies toward social egalitarianism, personal activism, and political fundamentalism." [21] He states a thesis relevant to the inquiry in these lectures: "a balance that ensures strong citadels of individual and group privacy and limits both disclosure and surveillance is a prerequisite for liberal democratic societies." [22]

We are confronted today with frightening enlargement of the technical means for invading privacy. Westin describes the technical apparatus for private and governmental physical surveillance (eavesdropping), for psychological surveillance (probing the mind by polygraph and personality testing), and for data collection and processing (accumulating information about individuals and private groups). For effective protection in a new technological setting of those interests in privacy that are essential for self-realization, all the old approaches in social technology for limiting and restraining administration in both public and private spheres

17. Published by Atheneum, N.Y., 1967.
18. Ibid. p. 7.
19. Ibid. p. 8.
20. Ibid. p. 19.
21. Ibid. p. 27.
22. Ibid. p 24.

will need to be employed. Judicial doctrines and remedies, legislation defining limits and remedies, and internal administrative devices for notice, hearing, and appeal are already being debated and adopted. Westin even suggests the utility of an ombudsman to check on the uses of one of the devices of psychological surveillance—the polygraph.[23]

The third front involves safeguarding the interests of the less privileged members of society. The real test under democratic morality of our devices for notice, hearing, fair forums of decision, and independent review is their availability to those least able to protect themselves. As Wallace Mendelson has said: "Every culture provides at least reasonably well for those at the top of its social order. The crucial test is how it treats those at the bottom." [24] Repeatedly in these lectures the inclusion of the interests of those at the bottom of the social scale in the protection of the administrative state has been set forth as test of democracy.

We may be in the dawn of a new period when the requirements for humane administration with respect to persons of low estate get the attention required by democratic morality. Walter Gellhorn carries us to a climactic point in his book when he talks about "the continuing need for an outside eye" on police administration, and the need for "municipal tribunes of the people," particularly in such areas as welfare administration and public housing. "The local administration of social welfare laws," he says, "must assuredly be one of the most disheartening works of man." [25] Likewise, the power of public housing agencies "inescapably accentuates the feelings of insecurity in already insecure persons." [26] The Supreme Court—in decisions in such diverse areas as racial discrimination, forced confessions, and the right to counsel

23. Ibid. pp. 240–41.
24. Wallace Mendelson, *Discrimination* (Englewood Cliffs, N.J.: Prentice-Hall, Inc., 1962), p. 1.
25. Gellhorn, *When Americans Complain,* p. 196.
26. Ibid. p. 207.

for one's defense—has made us conscious of the humane test of administration. The antipoverty program has initiated new ventures toward effective representation of the interests of the poor in administration. It has, on the one hand, done much to amplify notice to the poor and access by the poor to legal and other forums, even in some cases stirring the poor to the group organization that appears to be essential for effective representation of interests in the administrative state. It has, on the other hand, raised the question whether the gap between the professional elites who administer programs for the poor and the poor themselves can be bridged without participation by the poor in the forums of administration.

Students of administration have not looked with favor on participative democracy when it extended beyond advice and other forms of access to invasion of the forum of administration itself.[27] They should, however, be conscious of the fact that interests are represented inside the forums of decision and action in innumerable instances, extending from representation of bankers in the top-level Federal Reserve Board to representation of farmers in administration at the bottom of the administrative hierarchy. They should be conscious also of the fact that the issue is somewhat different when the social distance between the professionals who administer and the poor who are presumably served is as great as it is in America today. Moreover, participation is the basic requirement of democratic morality; and in the case of the poor, stimulation of participation in administration may be a

27. For an insightful discussion emphasizing the advisory role as the appropriate means of interest participation, see Walter Gellhorn, *Federal Administrative Proceedings* (Baltimore: The Johns Hopkins Press, 1941), Chapter IV. For a balanced and questioning view, see John M. Gaus, "The Citizen as Administrator," in Roscoe C. Martin, ed., *Public Administration and Democracy: Essays in Honor of Paul Appleby* (Syracuse, N.Y.: Syracuse University Press, 1965), Chapter IX. For a criticism of the recent trend toward "corporationalism," see Theodore Lowi, "The Public Philosophy: Interest-Group Liberalism," *The American Political Science Review*, Vol. LXI (March 1967), pp. 5–24.

means of encouraging and developing a more general participation in the affairs of society.

It is not surprising that these humanizing movements—
whether in the courts, in the antipoverty program, or in other
arenas—should stir controversy. The specific results of the
new movements may be obscured from our vision, but we
can hope and perhaps even expect that the fuller achievement
of democratic morality in the administration of programs
affecting the poor will be on the agenda of government in
the future.

VII

Man as Worker in Organization

ORGANIZATIONS ARE DEVELOPED to serve the interests of some kind of clientele or group of clienteles. The primary clientele to be served may be an internal one. This is true of consumer cooperatives, unions, and trade associations. It is true also of producer co-operatives—organizations that serve external clienteles but for the benefit of the internal organizing group. On the other hand, the clientele may be external to the organization. It may be a proprietor who, whether active in the organization or an absentee owner, is interested in extracting benefits for himself from the organization. Or it may be a public service organization serving consumer clienteles of some kind external to the organization. The organizations within the administrative state, except those performing managerial services for other organizations, are almost exclusively of this type. They do not exist to serve the needs of internal clienteles or proprietors, but for service to external clienteles whose interests are represented in roles defined for the organizations. The interests of these clienteles to be served by the organization are regarded as the governing set of primary values for the organization and are called its goals, purposes, or missions.

Almost always an additional set of interests is developed within an organization. The consumer co-operative, union, or producer co-operative employs workers who do not share equally (or who may not share at all) in the primary interests served by the organization. Likewise, proprietary firms and public service organizations must employ workers. These include a variety of persons ranging from the manual worker performing the most humble tasks to the top management of the organization. They may as subjects of the administrative state share in the diffused benefits of the organization, and they may accept the mission of the organization as the objective of their work. They also share with the clienteles served by the organization an interest in the survival and strength of the organization, and this mutuality of interest between workers inside and clienteles outside is a co-ordinating factor giving strength to organization and continuing unity in its operation. But they will, nevertheless, have personal and group interests as workers that are distinct from the service values of the organization or even from the instrumental value of organization survival. Moreover, there will be conflicts between the interests of workers and those of clienteles and between interests of various types of workers.

There is in this situation no new kind of quandary for democratic theory, but only a perplexing problem of application. In the view of democracy presented in these lectures, the interest of the worker is one among the types of interests to be served by the state. They are separable, high-quantity interests important to man's self-realization. But they are not the only interests to be served, nor indeed are they the primary ones. The attainment of each man's interests is dependent upon the ability of organizations to serve the multitude of clienteles of which he is a part. Workers will be poorly served if the interests of policemen, firemen, teachers, and other groups of workers are protected in ways that prevent good police protection, fire protection, service to students, and other benefits that are shared by the various clienteles of organizations. Hence consensus, reconciliation, and choice among interests, heretofore stated as routes to achievement of democratic morality, must be instruments of resolution in one other arena—that of man as worker in organization.

Traditional ideas in our culture have supported the supremacy of clientele interests in the employment relationship. In the prebureaucratic phase of capitalism when individuals were proprietors of enterprises using their capital, proprietary interests were sanctioned by law and prevailing concepts of moral right. As the organizational revolution began to develop the proprietary rights of individual owners were exercised by whatever persons managed the enterprise in the owner's interest. The parallel of these ideas in public affairs was the concept of sovereignty. The doctrine of state sovereignty preserved the supremacy of state interests in the same way that the concept of proprietor rights preserved the interests of the owner. Moreover, while in the foundations of constitutional government in the late Middle Ages a distinction was drawn between sovereign rights and the proprietary rights of monarchs, with respect to the employment relationship the state retained for itself both sovereign and proprietary rights. Hence in the nineteenth and twentieth centuries when rights of individuals in public employment were construed in due process and civil rights cases, the courts began with historic assumptions of complete state supremacy on matters of public employment. These traditional concepts have now been punctured repeatedly by legislation and judicial decisions, as will be shown later in this chapter, but the rubric of sovereignty has not been destroyed; it continues to influence policy.

The old ideas, which undoubtedly were responses to dominant interests at the time of their development, are now supported by new social interests. Technology and social interdependence have made all of us dependent upon the service of organizations. This is not merely a dependence on organizations in general, but also dependence upon particular organizations. The maintenance of organization service at some level of proficiency is often widely regarded as a social necessity, and if not this, then desirable for safeguarding many interests within society. The laws that deny or limit the right to strike in some way are indicative of this felt dependence on organizations.

The effect of this single example is to illustrate that laws and administrative practices that today maintain the rights of management in the employment relationship, while in accord with traditional concepts, are also responses to the current dependence of clienteles upon organizations for the promotion and preservation of their interests.

Workers must serve these clientele interests, for the essence of the employment relationship is a commitment of the worker to render his service for the purposes for which the organization presumably exists. The worker must accept and bow to the "mission" of the organization. Nevertheless, the self-attainment of the individual within the society will be dependent upon the recognition also of his interests in the employment relationship. Three kinds of interest can be distinguished. The first are material interests, including such things as number of hours of work, payment for work, physical conditions of work, and both opportunity for and security of employment. The second are psychic, and relate to the worker's status, including such things as the dignity lent by the work performed, his freedom from arbitrary exercise of authoritarian command, and a sense of being a respected and contributing member of the organization. The third are the worker's interests in privacy, that is, in preserving his concerns as a person from being excessively absorbed by the employment relationship.

Fulfillment of these interests can be prevented or compromised by the worker's subjection to organization. While organizations may provide men with opportunities for work, they may at the same time be harsh with respect to conditions of employment, material benefits, and severance of the employment relationship. Workers can be abused physically, humiliated, and robbed of their spirit; their initiative can be crushed, their self-development frustrated, and their independence as men destroyed.

There are factors in society which ameliorate the effects of worker subjection and others which heighten his dependence on the employing organization. Among the ameliorating factors the first has been the consensus against slavery and serfdom, then against brutality, then toward respect for the dignity of man. These developments—partly in law and partly in attitude—toward a humane society have come late, particularly the concern for the psychic well-being of the worker. They are buttressed by the economic power of worker organizations and the political power of workers. A further amelioration is the reduction in the hours of work and the concomitant opportunities of man to find self-satisfaction in the use of leisure. The man who cannot find gratifications in the employment relationship—who indeed may find drudgery and dejection there—may find richness of opportunity in his hours and days of leisure. C. Wright Mills thought that leisure values were replacing the "gospel of work" that characterized the Calvinistic ethic of the nation. Indeed, according to Mills, leisure "lends to work such meanings as work has." [1] Third, the level of human labor is being raised. Drudge work and menial labor are being eliminated by mechanization. An increasing percentage of employment requires some human ingenuity and expertness, and carries with it the dignity of middle-class employment.

Fourth, there is enough fluidity in modern society to allow much choice of occupation and also ability to rise in the scale of employment opportunities. Fifth, the requirements for expertness reduce the subjection of the worker to those in

1. *White Collar: The American Middle Classes* (New York, N.Y.: Oxford University Press, 1956), p. 236.

"command" positions. Organizations are so dependent upon the co-operative activity of the diverse groups of experts within them that the command functions of the superstructures are limited. This is peculiarly evident at the topmost levels, but the dependence reaches deep into the organization. College administrators have limited ability to command teachers; so-called directors of scientific organizations are dependent upon the co-operative meshing of the knowledge of the scientists in the organization; generals and their counterparts at lower levels find that co-ordinative functions replace command functions as means of integrating the technical specialists on which they are dependent; administrators in varied types of organizations are dependent on those who know how to operate computers and other mechanized equipment. Those who have expertness have professional attitudes —what Thorstein Veblen loosely called an "instinct of workmanship"—and those who deal with them in the name of organizations must come to terms both with their knowledge and with their attitudes. The result is that the nature of authority changes—it is less a power to command than to co-ordinate.[2] And the position of the worker changes—because of his possession of expert skills, his dependence is decreased and his dignity and sense of worth are raised.

There are countervailing factors that may keep the worker dependent. Since the opportunities of most men for remunerative self-employment are limited or nonexistent, they are dependent upon a job in an organization. This dependence is on the type of organization that can use a given skill, and for millions of men it becomes by middle age dependence upon a single organization. In such a case man's dependence is somewhat akin to that of serfdom, the attachment being to an organization rather than to the land. The degree of this dependence is, of course, determined by the many fac-

2. Of the considerable amount of literature on this point, particular note should be taken of Victor A. Thompson, *Modern Organization* (New York: Alfred A. Knopf, 1961).

tors which affect the mobility of the worker—the condition of the economy, the demand for his specialization, his age and skill, and so on.

A further factor is the capacity of organizations for engrossment of individuals. They can engross more of a man than forty or sixty hours of work per week. William H. Whyte, Jr., tried to tell us what happens to a man who gets ahead in organizations. He is absorbed, thought Whyte, into a "social ethic" of "belongingness," which means, "He is to adjust to the group rather than vice versa"; of "togetherness," which means envelopment of the individual in "group work"; and of "scientism," which means the use of social science to engineer consent—public relations and personnel counseling will make him "feel himself part of a larger movement." [3] Men as workers and as co-operators with other organizations of which they are members "have left home, spiritually as well as physically, to take the vows of organization life." [4] Whyte did not think the individual could escape the collective spirit merely by membership in many organizations, but he did believe that the individual's autonomy could be partially preserved by avoiding, in Clark Kerr's words, "total involvement in any organization." [5]

It is, of course, the subjection to the single organization for which a person works that concerns us here. Such an organization may gain a grip over a man's existence. Westin, whose discussion of invasions of citizen privacy has already been discussed, summarizes vividly the ways in which physical surveillance, personality testing, the polygraph, and data collection are used by employers—including agencies of the national government—in selection and retention of employees.[6] Yet these devices are supplemented by others to win

---

3. William H. Whyte, Jr., *The Organization Man* (Garden City, N.Y.: Doubleday & Compny, Inc., 1957), Chapters 3, 4, and 5.
4. Ibid. p. 3.
5. Ibid. pp. 50–51.
6. *Supra,* pp. 150–51.

loyalty to the organization. It may aim toward socialization of the worker to the group norms dominant in the organization and may achieve this to the extent (or in such ways) that his competence and will for constructive individual initiative are destroyed or seriously impaired. The sacrifice of individual independence to the organization may be especially destructive of the worker's spirit if he thinks that the internal norms of the organization which dictate his socialization are unrelated to, or even have displaced, the service role of the organization. General socialization within the society may have prepared him for subordination to the public service role of the organization but not for the internal norms of organization life.

In addition, an organization may seek control over the extra-employment activities of the employee. To hold his job many a public school teacher must forfeit his rights as a man and a citizen, and similar constraint exists in varying degrees of intensity for many who, for example, become corporate executives, join law firms, or become members of the medical profession. The forfeiture may not be conscious or may not bother the man who is indifferent to the issue of personal independence, but it may prove a traumatic experience for others. In either case, the issue is presented: can a man be a good employee and at the same time remain also both a free man and a good citizen?

It is fruitless to try to evaluate whether the ameliorations or the curtailments of man's integrity of person and spirit weigh more heavily in the balances between opportunity and restriction. One must be concerned, however, over the conflict of interests between clienteles and the organizations established to serve them on the one hand, and the interests of men who work for the organizations on the other. He must be interested in the problems of choice and reconciliation between the conflicting interests.

Authoritarianism

Four kinds of answers to the problems arising from man as worker in organization can be discerned. The first and readiest answer is *authoritarianism*. It has its roots in traditional concepts and was inherent in what some have called the classical theory of organization. In its original and extreme form it was *absolutist authoritarianism*. It assumed the absolute right in employer-employee relations of the proprietor or the sovereign, and of the directorates, managers, and supervisors who represented him. Even now the doctrine has its champions. Thus a businessman says: "It is my business; I have the right to decide who my employees will be." A school board member declares, "A teacher has no right to teach or to act outside the classroom contrary to our directions." An authoritarian executive states, "They will carry out my orders or they can work somewhere else."

The instrumental device for implementing authoritarian claims in organizations has been hierarchical command and supervision. As organizations arose and expanded, the interests of the proprietor and the sovereign, and of the concerned clienteles as well, were delegated down a hierarchical line, with each level of workers being governed by the directives from the levels above them. Organizational theory, in its classical form, centered on hierarchy as the instrument of service to those who possessed the ultimate rights.

No one has yet shown how the interests of clienteles served by large public organizations, given the inescapable layering characteristic of these structures, can be protected and promoted without some translation of clientele interests into rights of hierarchical command over workers in the organizations. Subordination of the worker function to clientele interests seems unavoidable, and hence some subordination of the worker to the hierarchies presumably representing the clientele interests. Yet absolutism has been forsaken both in the public policy of the nation and in the practice of enlightened management. The old tradition, and the rights of clienteles served by organization, is preserved in *moderated authoritarianism*. The authoritarianism may be moderated by any or all of the other three answers to the problem of man as worker in organization.

Guildism

The second answer is *guildism*. In a revolutionary form, guildism asks for the radical transfer of the rights of management to the workers or their direct representatives. This might be sought with retention of large organization, in which case the worker's subjection to hierarchical command would not be eliminated—though he might feel it was not an alien command. It might be sought, as it was in the proposals of some guild socialists, in a more radical attack on the administered society—a reorganization of work into independent factory or small group units controlled by the workers acting co-operatively rather than under subjection to order.[7] This kind of proposal looks toward the fullest realization of workers' democracy and the fullest emancipation of the worker from subjection to others. It does not appear to be an achievable objective, because it runs counter to the modern trend toward centralism. It seems even more utopian than proposals for radical decentralization of industry to the extent necessary to make pure market theory operable, or for radical decentralization of government to the extent necessary to create full local control of services. Centralism, with accompanying large organization and hierarchy, is apparently part of the inexorable forces of modern history in the making.

7. For an exposition of decentralized guildism, see G. D. H. Cole, *Guild Socialism Re-Stated* (London: Leonard Parsons, 1920), especially Chapter III. Compare Erich Fromm, *The Sane Society* (New York: Rinehart & Co., Inc., 1955), pp. 321ff.

The revolutionary guild ideal may seek only a halfway position through workers' comanagement. A notable attempt toward this in our day is in Yugoslavia. The Yugoslavs have tried to combine representation of workers' interests and community interests through shared management. But we are offered here some substantiation for the hypothesis that decentralization will be accompanied by centralization; for while workers are given participation in selection of management, they are still subject to such central controls as are exerted through the party mechanisms and the central banking and taxing and subsidy operations of the national and state governments.[8]

These revolutionary proposals for liberation and realization for the worker do not offer the degree of hope in the world of realities that their proponents assume. First, size—and hence hierarchy—and unequal capacities and inclinations of men for participation would impose the usual limitations on democratic participation in the administered society. While complete oligarchy could presumably be avoided and the reality of worker participation increased, limitations on participation would still exist. Second, neither the drudgery nor the routine nature of some work would be eliminated, and the humiliation of subordinate status for those performing such tasks would remain. Third, guild action in practice normally seeks motivation for work in rewards to workers rather than in a sense of purpose for performance of work.[9] The appeal of guild socialism lies in its proposal to transfer rewards from one supplier interest to another—from the proprietors and managers representing them to workers and managers representative of their interests. It can be attacked in the realm of government services

8. For an argument for comanagement as a route to "Humanistic Communitarian Socialism," presented as the alternative to what is called the *"robotism"* of both the capitalist and communist varieties, see Erich Fromm, *The Sane Society*, pp. 323ff. and 363.

9. For an argument that comanagement is for this reason "sociological conservatism," see John H. Schaar, *Escape from Authority: The Perspectives of Erich Fromm* (New York: Basic Books, 1961), Chapter IV.

as retrogressive in that it submerges the idea that the motivation of work is the service to be rendered by the performance of the work.

Finally, guild action on a revolutionary scale accentuates, and perhaps makes unmanageable, the task of reconciliation of interests. Comanagement assumes a rival interest with which the interest of the worker is to be shared. The structuralization of the two interests for coparticipation brings the two into direct confrontation and may produce conflict rather than the co-operation assumed in utopian guildism. Reconciliation may be possible, as in Yugoslavia, only through some external centralization. Complete control of economic production by workers would present even greater problems of co-ordination between the structure for work and the structure for representation of clientele interests. Theoretical guild socialists and syndicalists have recognized the need for reconciling these two sets of interests through a two-house parliament or some other structural device. It is clear, however, that a corporately organized society, whether on the basis of proprietor or worker organizations, would be difficult to manage, both for resolution of conflicts among producer organizations and for representation of shared interests in common services.

We must take note, however, of the evolutionary development toward representation of workers' interests through limited guild action. Workers' organizations now bargain collectively with management in the private sector and national law has protected rights of organization and collective action. Workers' organizations are now prevalent, also, in the public service. Some of these bargain collectively with public agencies; others—witness the postal workers—work through political channels to obtain their objectives. Some, like the teachers, are resorting both to political action and the strike.[10]

Usually these organizations have been interested primarily

10. Chapter VI of the study by Frederick C. Mosher, cited earlier, is titled "The Collective Services." It treats "limited guild action" in more detail than is possible here.

or exclusively in material rewards for their members. Sometimes, as in the case of teachers' unions or professional organizations, they have sought additional ends which they identified with the service interests of clienteles. This is true of the battle of teachers for academic freedom. Sometimes also they have sought participation in the making of policy. This is true particularly in colleges, where teachers insist on participation in the making of educational policy, and even in the choice of the administrators under whom they will serve. In April 1967 the welfare workers in New York City made a demand for participation in the administrative development of welfare policies. For professionals in organizations today, there is a certain built-in tendency toward guildism in the dependence of managers upon the co-operation of several types of specialists in the organization.

Limited guild action is probably a necessary part of the democratic answer to the problem of man as worker in organization. It protects the interests of workers, and it may contribute to the more effective rendering of service. Nevertheless it presents some difficult problems of policy and administration. One problem is that of the strike of public employees. Usually prohibited by law, the strike is nevertheless being used increasingly. No other dilemma reflects more clearly the conflict between worker interests and clientele interests. Another problem is the ever-present personal and professional stakes of workers who participate in policy making. I have already referred to the existence of these stakes in the deliberations of college faculties over educational policy.[11] Perhaps my own university's recent decision to allow the student association to nominate three students to serve with voting rights on the Educational Policies Committee exemplifies a larger need than that of worker participation— namely, clientele representation. At least the move shows recognition of the potential conflict between guildism and clientele service.

11. See pages 143–44.

Human Relations

The third answer to the problem identified above is called *human relations*. In the human relations approach attention is directed to the needs, expectations, and motivations of the worker in organizations. While guildism is one means for assertion of workers' interests, human relations offers a greater variety of instrumental approaches.

In its origins it was a corrective for assumptions and techniques of the scientific management movement which originated with Frederick W. Taylor. It made no attack on the traditional assumption that work should serve the interests of management and of clienteles represented by it; but it brought into question the materialistic assumptions and mechanistic techniques of Taylorism. Taylorism assumed that the carrot of material reward was sufficient motivation, and that with this motivation workers could be directed and controlled like machine parts in a production line. Work could be prescribed in detail, time and motion studies made to determine performance and piecework remuneration, and tight supervision provided to ensure high productivity. Taylor was, it should be noted, dealing with routine functions, and hence could say that the worker was "not to increase production by his own initiative, but to perform punctiliously the orders given down to their slightest detail." [12]

The deficiencies of the scientific management approach were revealed in the Hawthorne studies, made at the Western Electric Company's plant bearing that name, from 1927 to 1932.[13] These and other studies provided evidence that the worker's production rate was set by social norms rather than physiological capacity. The group determined the production

12. The quotation is from Robert T. Golembiewski, *Men, Management, and Morality: Toward a New Organizational Ethic* (New York: McGraw-Hill Book Co., 1965), p. 162.

13. For reports on the studies, see Elton Mayo, *The Human Problems of an Industrial Civilization* (New York: The Macmillan Company, 1933), and F. J. Roethlisberger and W. J. Dickson, *Management and the Worker* (Cambridge, Mass.: Harvard University Press, 1939).

standard. These studies gave impetus to other inquiries on motivation of workers, socialization within small groups, and leadership attuned to worker motivation through influence on group standards. In brief, attention was redirected from mechanistic approaches, material rewards, and tight command to human factors, group effort, and leadership techniques that promoted morale and initiative.

"Human relations" was the name given to a new way of thought about management-worker relationships. The new approach was reflected in an enormous amount of empirical study on such things as human motivation and small group action. It generated emphasis on normative standards which were man-centered. Human values in the work relationship have been asserted; self-actualization of the worker through democratic work processes has been stated as a goal; and recently an author has supported the approach as one means of implementing the Judeo-Christian ideology.[14] Yet management "rights" have not been forgotten, and frequently one cannot tell whether an author writing on human relations is more interested in workers or in greater productivity, or whether he is assuming a complete harmony between the interests of workers and the interests of management.

While the content of the empirically based and normative literature on human relations is richly diversified, three general aspects of it are distinguishable. One is the attitude on the exercise of authority. The right to command is softened into a concept of adjustive leadership and supervision. The exercise of management is to be adjusted to the needs and aspirations of workers. Management is to be employee-centered. The effective manager and the moral manager will be sensitive to employee stakes and motivations. He will provide adequate material compensation along with hygienic conditions of work, be considerate of employee feelings, and be fair and nonpunitive in all his dealings with employees.

14. Golembiewski, *Men, Management, and Morality.*

Supervision should be general rather than tight, and leadership through communication of purpose should be substituted for command.

A second characteristic of the literature is emphasis on the sharing of power and responsibility. Decision making should be shared by delegation and by group participation. Decentralization and participative management are goals to be sought because they tap the initiative, creativeness, and talent of subordinates, and enlarge their satisfaction in work and dignity as persons. The third aspect is emphasis in some of the literature on self-actualization of the worker. The goal is the development of the personality of the worker so that he may share in the realization of the highest values that can be developed out of the work relationship. This aspect of the human relations approach will be elaborated more fully presently.

In the meantime, the general characteristic of and the variations in the human relations approach should be examined. Its general tendency and flavor is humanistic and democratic. Nevertheless, we can distinguish certain variations (or shadings) in purpose or emphasis among those who advocate the human relations answer to the problem of man as worker in organization. While conscious of the pitfalls and limitations of classification of ideas diversely expressed, I shall distinguish three shadings of human relations thought. At the same time, I shall indicate the dualism in purpose— interest in both management service of clientele purposes and worker needs—that, in spite of the variations, is normally reflected in human relations thought and in the movement toward human relations in management practice.

The first variation can be called *managerial conservationalism*. In this variation human relations is a tool of effective management. There is no attack upon the traditional assumption that organizations exist to serve clienteles and that management should marshal the activities of workers to serve the purposes of clienteles. Managers will, therefore, use techniques of leadership which are employee-centered and will delegate responsibilities and employ group participation because these things are effective techniques of management—techniques which contribute to the fulfillment of the clientele (or clientele-management) purposes of the organization. This is the point of view that is dominant in management textbooks and treatises which have as their purpose the development of effective managers.[15]

Yet this simple description of motivations does not fully explain the behavior of modern management. Management's primary objective is compromised by acceptance of workers' needs, producing a dualism in perspective. On the one hand, the human relations approach has become part of the general ethic of society, and managers are influenced by the deposit of human relations ideas to the extent that these may be accepted in practice without constant consideration of management advantage. On the other hand, the manager must be interested in whether there are payoffs to the organization in group participation, delegation, or other devices. Moreover, the empirical data developed in human relations studies can be used for manipulative purposes. Thus, for example, the knowledge on personality testing can be used as a means for recruiting and promoting persons who can most readily be socialized into the spirit and habits of the organization.

The second variation of the human relations approach can be called *moderate humanism*. In this variation primary emphasis is placed on the development and use of worker capacity, and management is asked to accommodate its practices to this objective. Yet management is not asked to sacrifice the objectives of effective organizational service and its accommodation to worker needs is to be achieved largely through structural arrangements.

15. For an example, see Rensis Likert, *New Patterns of Management* (New York: McGraw-Hill Book Co., Inc., 1966). But for reaction against full acceptance, see George Strauss, "Some Notes on Power-Equalization," in Harold J. Leavitt, *The Social Science of Organizations: Four Perspectives* (Englewood Cliffs, N.J.: Prentice-Hall, Inc., 1963), pp. 39–84.

This variation of human relations is reflected in a recent book by Golembiewski on *Men, Management, and Morality*.[16] Golembiewski desires that the Judeo-Christian humanistic ethic be embodied in the practice of organizations. He believes the empirical data that have been developed show ways that this can be done. He attacks the use by management of human relations techniques developed in this data for manipulative purposes. He believes, however, that it is possible to mesh personality and organization, that is, to promote both human needs and effective management. There is, in other words, a dualism in perspective, in spite of the primary emphasis on human needs. The means of attaining "individual freedom in organizations while serving organization purposes" include such things as self-choice by the worker in job assignments, job enlargement for the worker, job enlargement for supervisors, broad span of control, supervisory techniques that increase independence of the workers, group decision making, and decentralization. By and large, the techniques suggested are structural adaptations, are moderate in scope, and assume a compatibility between workers' needs and organizational needs.

The third variation may be called *radical humanism* or, alternatively, *psychological humanism*. The radical humanist seeks more than adaptation of organization to workers; he wants to provide the environment that will lead toward worker growth and behavior in accord with highest values. This is sometimes referred to as "changing people," meaning the guidance of their behavior toward the development of healthy personalities. Herbert A. Shepard, for example, distinguishes between the "primary mentality" and the "secondary mentality." The former is self-centered: "The individual is separated from the rest of the world by his skin. What goes on inside the skin gives meaning to the terms survival and well-being." The latter finds "growth" "in the expansion of self to include others." The individual "can develop and

16. Cited above.

express his full potential [in an] interpersonal relationship." The primary mentality sees a personal threat in interpersonal relations, but the secondary personality sees opportunity for actualizing his needs through his relations with others. The pattern of management that accords with the former is coercion, and compromise of separate interests; the pattern that accords with the latter is collaboration and consensus.[17]

Another example of the "change in people" perspective is offered in Chris Argyris's explanation of the conflicting sets of characteristics of mature persons and children. Management may coerce people into the dependent and submissive position of the latter, or support their development toward independence, lack of passivity, and other qualities of a mature person.[18] In another approach, the psychologist Alexander Maslow has provided an hierarchical structure of needs that are required for full development. Arranged from highest to lowest they include the following: self-actualization needs, status or prestige needs, self-esteem needs, belongingness or love needs, safety needs, and physiological needs.[19]

Some people will regard the ideal of "expansion of self to include others," or of development of the mature personality, or of satisfying all of the psychological needs of the worker as utopian goals for organization—as extending beyond what is the feasible or legitimate purpose of organizations serving external clienteles. Implementation of the ideals stated by Shepard is being sought through the so-called laboratory approach, particularly in T-groups, in training employees in interpersonal relations. Such training may have value for management as well as for the worker, but will not eliminate the need for correlation of the activities of the workers with

17. Herbert A. Shepard, "Changing Interpersonal and Intergroup Relationships in Organizations," in James G. March, ed., *Handbook of Organizations* (Chicago: Rand McNally & Company, 1965), pp. 1115–43.
18. See Chris Argyris, "The Individual and Organization," *Administrative Science Quarterly*, Vol. IV (September 1959), pp. 145–67.
19. See Alexander Maslow, *Toward a Psychology of Being* (Princeton, N.J.: D. Van Nostrand Company, Inc., 1962), pp. 23–24.

the purpose of the organization. Shepard notes that the collaboration-consensus system requires not only commitment of employees to one another, but also to superordinate goals. This is acceptance of an old idea of management, namely that workers should be motivated by communication of the substantive purpose of organization.[20] This too resurrects the central issue: What interests are to be served by organizations? Must collaboration and consensus be achieved by worker acceptance of external goals—and coercive management, or at least compromise management, be accepted where the interests of workers and the external goals are not fully compatible?

What conclusions can be drawn from this analysis of the human relations approach to an old dilemma? Three sets of observations are relevant to the issues identified. They are presented from the dualism in perspective that is normal, which Argyris has so aptly referred to as the desirability of means "by which the individual actualizes himself through the organization and simultaneously the organization actualizes itself through the individual." [21] But I do not assume that this ideal is fully realizable: the individual is only partially actualized through his work relationship, and there will be conflicts between his purposes and organization purposes as interpreted by top management.

The first observation is that the prime purpose of public organizations is to serve external interests and that workers must accept this as fact. If a professor does not have the competence to teach or does not apply himself to the task, he has no moral right to ask the American Association of University Professors to protect his tenure. If a policeman is unwilling to accept the possibility that his job may endanger his life, he should not be a policeman. For many of us, compatibility with the organization we serve is fostered by the

20. See Chester I. Barnard, *The Functions of the Executive* (Cambridge. Mass.: Harvard University Press, 1938).
21. Argyris, "The Individual and Organization," p. 146.

opportunities we have had for self-choice: of the kind of work we wanted to do, the kind of organization we wanted to work in, and even the job assignment in that organization. We may also have some opportunity to move to another organization. But we will all be frustrated in some way—whether by belief the organization is not serving its purpose adequately, through feeling that we are not being used effectively, or for another reason.

Second, both kinds of objectives sought in the dual perspective may be achieved by development and use of talent within an organization. Career development from bottom to top of an organization—equipping men for enlargement of their contribution—can serve the interests of both the organization and the worker. And in modern organizations the desire of workers to participate is paralleled by the organizational need for co-operation in decision making and operations from diffuse centers. Effective interpersonal relations in shared tasks, and management that co-ordinates the capacities of men with complementary competencies are necessities of management; they also broaden the sense of participation and contribution.

Nevertheless, while there is parallelism in organizational and personal needs, there is no possibility of complete identification. All cannot rise on the career ladder who want to rise, and all cannot participate to the extent and in the manner they wish. There are frustrations for men in organizations, and requirements for their adaptations to their own limitations and bad fortune—as in other aspects of life. And there is something more than status symbols separating those who achieve and those who do not; there is the consciousness that men are on different rungs of a performance ladder— that selective assignment of duties discriminates among men and enhances or limits opportunities for self-contribution.

Third, while organizational objectives call for adaptations and some submissiveness from workers, organizations through their management must also adapt to workers—not merely for organizational reasons but because of the ideal of a humane society. Harshness, indignities to men, engrossment of their private lives, and lack of empathy for their material and psychological needs are inconsistent with the democratic morality as it was described in Chapter I. Organizations may be asked to serve values which do not further—indeed, may conflict with—the prime purpose for their existence. They may be barred, for example, from racial discrimination in employment practices, without regard to whether or not this contributes to attainment of the fundamental objective of the organization. We may be witnessing now the beginnings of a significant new demand on organizations—a demand that private organizations take on the "human relations" function of training unemployed ghetto inhabitants for remunerative employment; in effect organizations would then be changing the patterns of the lives of the people by equipping them with capacities for self-realization, in accord with the standards of self-realization prevailing in the society.

Liberal Constitutionalism

Mention of the possibility that organizations may be required to serve values in conflict with (or apart from) their prime purpose leads to the fourth approach to the dilemma of the conflict between organizational and worker values. It may be called *liberal constitutionalism*. It contemplates legal definition of the rights of and limitations on the parties in the employment relationship.

This approach is reflected in the growing public law governing employment in the private sector. Let us note some of the elements in this expansion of public law. To the owner and manager the law says: you shall not make a man a slave or subject him to involuntary servitude; you shall not fire him or refuse to employ him because he is a member of a union; you shall not discriminate against a prospective or employed worker because of his race, color, sex, or age; you shall not abuse his person contrary to the law of the land;

you shall maintain healthy and safe working conditions; you shall pay taxes for unemployment, retirement, and disability insurance for the worker. Absolutism in the employment relation has been denied by the laws of the land. And to the worker the law says: there are limitations on guildism—on strikes, picketing, and related matters.

The approach is reflected sharply in the rules relating to employment in the service of the administrative state. There are, of course, rules on the rights of those in the military services; but I shall illustrate the expansion of liberal constitutionalism by reference to the areas dealt with in civil service law applicable to the national government's employees. It will be understood that this is a rapidly expanding body of law and hence that issues in some of these areas are not finally resolved. The list, although not all-inclusive, is sufficient to show the extent of use of the approach called liberal constitutionalism. There are rules on

1. Material rewards, including compensation rates, overtime or night or holiday work, coffee breaks, annual and sick leaves, maternity leaves, health benefits, group insurance, and retirement benefits;

2. Tenure rights, including those with respect to reductions in force, re-employment, restoration after military duty, suspension, and terminations;

3. Developmental opportunities, including those for training and eligibility for new job assignments;

4. Discrimination on the basis of age, sex, race, or color, or political affiliation;

5. Loyalty and security tests, including substantive limitations on these and procedural safeguards against their misuse or overextension;

6. Conflicts of interests;

7. Unionization, including rights to join unions, to present views through unions to executive

and congressional authorities, and in some cases to bargain on employee benefits;

8. Political participation—involving reconciliation of the employee's rights to freedom from coercion in his participation as a citizen with the needs of the government for political neutrality of employees;

9. Individual petition and presentation of information to Congress and other authorities;

10. Veterans' rights in employment;

11. Initiation, presentation, and processing of grievances; and

12. Appeal procedures.

Constitutionalism, in this narrow sense of the organic law governing relationships, is obviously one of the ways the interests of workers in organizations are safeguarded, promoted, and balanced with other interests. It can be a part of a broader constitutionalism governing the behavior of organizations toward men within them—a broader constitutionalism which includes, in addition to the organic law, the countervailing power of guild organizations against clientele and clientele/management-oriented organizations, the management science that instructs management on the means of developing the human resources within organizations, and a social consensus on the dignity of man as a value limiting and impelling the behavior of men in strategic positions of authority toward other men. This concept of a broader constitutionalism will be familiar to the student of government who thinks of the constitutionalism of the political system in terms of organic rules, countervailing powers, the official roles of men in strategic positions, and the public opinion that provides a consensus for the regime.[22]

---

22. The concept of constitutionalism is being reanalyzed for its applicability to the private sector. See Richard Eells, *The Government of Corporations* (New York: Free Press of Glencoe, 1962), and Emmette S. Redford, "Business as Government," in Roscoe C. Martin, ed., *Public Administration and Democracy: Essays in Honor of Paul H. Appleby* (Syracuse, N.Y.: Syracuse University Press, 1965), pp. 63–82.

SUMMARY

The answer to the problem of man as worker in organization, approached from the ideals of the democratic morality, will be eclectic. Organizations are created in the administrative state to serve external (clientele) interests, which are in varying degrees high-quantity or low-quantity interests; men working within them have high-quantity interests. From our empirical knowledge we cannot assume complete congruency between the external and the internal interests. The primacy of the mission of the organization—that is, of its external service objective—is asserted in the act of its creation, and will be legitimized under democratic morality if such acts of creation are the result of an interaction process responsive to the variety of interests in the community.

But the coexistence of the internal interests, and the high-quantity nature of these interests, prevent acceptance of absolutism in the employment relationship. For absolutism, it is necessary to substitute the concept of moderated authoritarianism. The moderation may come through guildism, in which workers—either by direct action within the organization or by political action—gain representation of their interests. It may come through human relations in management, either because management sees an identity in organizational objectives and workers' motivations or because the ideals of a humane society have been accepted as limitation of managerial authority, or both. Finally, the moderation may come through liberal constitutionalism, in which humane ideals are embodied in formal rules. It can be safely assumed that man as worker in organization can have his interests protected adequately in no one of these ways alone, but in the combination of all, producing an eclectic and broad constitutionalism for the worker.

VIII

The Administrative State in Perspective

MAN, WE HAVE SEEN, is subordinate to decisions made in and
actions taken through institutions. He is not born "in a
natural state" subject to nature alone, but in an administered
society where numerous organizations allocate advantages
and disadvantages to him. Many of these are public organizations. We have seen that there is an administrative state
consisting of numerous specialized organizations operating
with extremely complex and diversified internal and external
influences.

Let us look further at this system from perspectives which
overarch its particulars and raise the most meaningful questions for modern man. Why do we have the administrative
state? What is, after all, its essence? And what can make it
legitimate? When we have answered these questions we will
have rounded the circle back to the original inquiry with
which this book began.

WHY THE ADMINISTRATIVE STATE?

Basically, the administrative state exists because there are
shared needs that cannot be taken care of—either at all or
in the scope and in ways that are considered satisfactory—
without the continuing activity of public organizations. It

179

expands because our numbers, our proximity, our expectations, our society's affluence, and our capabilities for personal realization through joint action to meet shared needs increase in the complicated, technological civilization in which we live. Yet there are, in old ideology which still persists and in new ideology now gaining attention, three concepts which tell us that we should limit the administrative state, that perhaps we can limit it, and that perhaps also there are better routes to democracy than embrace of its discretion. What are these suggested routes and what validity is there in the claims made for them?

The first is the concept of laissez-faire or of "old individualism." It asserts that the welfare of all is best protected by the free assertion of the enterprise of each. It is a doctrine of self-help. Although embraced completely only by anarchists, it is widely and influentially asserted, even today, as doctrine that should limit the advance of the administrative state. For this purpose it is normally characterized as a regime of "free enterprise."

While presumably none of us would want to make the power of the state absolute over the enterprise of man, substantial practical limitations on our acceptance of the laissez-faire, or free-enterprise, concept can be stated in the form of three propositions.

First, escape from the administrative state would not mean escape from the administered society. The latter is ubiquitous and exists in both public and private sectors: for the business of society, the *whole* of society, is conducted by organizations with specialized functions.[1] On the private side,

1. From the voluminous writings on the effects of organization in the economy, reference may be made to Kenneth E. Boulding, *The Organizational Revolution* (New York: Harper & Row, 1953); Adolph A. Berle, Jr., *The 20th Century Capitalist Revolution* (New York: Harcourt, Brace & World, Inc., 1954); Wilbert E. Moore, *The Conduct of the Corporation* (New York: Random House, Inc., 1962); John Kenneth Galbraith, *The New Industrial State* (Boston: Houghton Mifflin Company, 1967); and Michael D. Reagan, *The Managed Economy* (New York: Oxford University Press, 1963).

organizations—corporations, unions, associations—are now the dominant factor in the economy. Man must live within them if he is to be sustained by his own employment, and he must buy from them and borrow from them if he is to enjoy even the minimum essentials of life. Their policies and managerial decisions—on production, wages, prices, advertising, etc.—allocate advantages and disadvantages to men. Man is, in other words, inescapably a subject of private administration.

Second, the ballot of the market place does not provide to man an adequate means of protecting and promoting his interests. Man casts his ballot much more frequently in the market place than he does in the political system. He votes when he chooses a product, or elects to buy or not to buy, to sell or not to sell, to borrow or not to borrow, to patronize one dealer rather than another. Yet in spite of the multitude of individual ballots, continuously cast, there are grave limitations on the capacity of the economic vote:

1. It cannot provide many common services desired by all or by significant groups.

2. It cannot correct abuses and injustices in the operation of the economic system.

3. It cannot deal successfully with the interrelationships and the interdependencies within the economy.

4. Money is the usual means of economic balloting and the lack of it deprives many of the ability to vote.

Anyone who looks at this list can make an extensive inventory of functions of government that have arisen because of inadequacies of the ballot in the market place. Man has turned to politics and to creation of the administrative state because his ballot in the market place did not satisfy all of his interests.

Third, the public and the private sectors of the administered society are interlocked. The private sector is dependent
upon the public, just as the public sector is dependent upon
the private. The private sector is propped and serviced in
innumerable ways by the administrative state. This has been
true historically as government guaranteed property and contract, granted licenses, maintained police and armies, and
supplied common services. It is much more true today as the
dependence on public services increases; the licensing of
trades, professions, and businesses expands; the dependence
on successful macroeconomic policies for the growth and
stability of the economy grows; and joint efforts of business
and government ramify into more and more fields—such as
is revealed by the science-military-industrial complex, the
public-private health complex, private housing construction
with public guarantees, and the many regulatory and pro-
motive activities of government with respect to particular
industries.

We could not retreat from the administrative state without
undermining the private sector of the administered society.
Nor could we back out of it without undermining numerous
benefits that groups of people, and sometimes all the people,
value too highly to relinquish. Moreover, the administrative
state continues to expand because balloting in the private
sector cannot give people all the benefits they desire and
because the rendering of the benefits they seek by political
balloting requires public administration. *The administrative
state will continue to expand because politicians see that
people have interests that can be fulfilled only by public
policy and its public administration.*

A second concept is a mixed system of public and private
enterprise, or, stated differently, public-private federalism.[2]

2. The concept of public-private federalism was apparently first advanced in
Don K. Price, "The Scientific Establishment," *Proceedings of the American
Philosophical Society*, Vol. CVI (June 1962), pp. 235–45. Analysis of the American economy as a mixed system is given in my *American Government and
the Economy* (New York: The Macmillan Company, 1965), Chapter II.

This assumes neither a totalitarian state nor an independent private sector, but a sharing of functions between the two. It assumes that self-help will be supplemented by an elaborate structure of both private and public organizations, each responding to man's interests.

The concept, stated either as mixed system or as public-private federalism, more accurately describes our administered society than either the concept of the administrative state or that of free enterprise. The accuracy of the description can perhaps best be illustrated by comparing it in four respects to the familiar federalism within our political system. The public position in the public-private federalism is similar to the national position in our national-state federalism.

First, just as the policy of the nation guides in national-state federalism, so the policy of the public or political arena guides in the public-private federalism. For the economy, public rules on antitrust, collective bargaining, minimum labor standards, quality or advertising of products, and other matters, determine the basic rules of the economic game.

Second, just as Morton Grodzins and Daniel Elazar have demonstrated that there is some national-state co-operation in every field of government activity,[3] so we can see that the functions of the public and private sectors are concurrent in every area of human activity. In national defense, education, health, housing, welfare, and other areas the functions are shared by public and private institutions. The postal service depends upon private transportation facilities; the enforcement of the law depends heavily upon private attorneys and much private policing; and in the private sector even religious practices are supported by police protection and tax exemption and are regulated by public rules on monogamy and many other matters affecting public order and morality. No activity is exclusively public or private.

Third, just as in national-state relations, so in the public-

3. See Morton Grodzins, *The American System: A New View of Government in the United States* (Chicago: Rand McNally & Company, 1966), edited by Daniel J. Elazar.

private arena there are complex power interrelationships between the concurrent authorities.

Fourth, just as national jurisdiction continues to expand
into functions which previously were primarily those of state
governments, so public functions expand into areas which
once were primarily or exclusively private. There are two
reasons why the latter tendency exists.[4] The first is that the
public jurisdiction is more comprehensive than that of any
private forum or set of forums. It can make rules that deal
with interdependencies, that cut across arenas within the
private sector, and that reflect the largest priorities in popular
demand. The second is that it can claim to be more representative. It can assert that in spite of all the imperfections
in attainment of the democratic ideal, the President and
Congress operating together in the solar system of politics
can be more representative of the total complex of conflicting and concurrent interests than General Motors, AFL-CIO,
or any other private structure in the administered society—
that, in other words, public policy and the administrative
state can be more democratic than private policy and administration.

Two hypotheses may be offered here: first, that power to
make policy on the basic felt needs of the people of a nation
will gravitate toward the most comprehensive jurisdiction;
and second, that such power will gravitate to the most democratic centers within the society. This is to say, combining
the hypotheses, that *comprehensive, democratic jurisdiction
attracts power.*

If the two hypotheses are valid, and if the political power
is indeed more representative than any other, then we can
expect the administrative state to continue to expand within
the administered society. This is not to suggest, as a norma-

4. See the discussion of these two factors in the writings of Paul Appleby in
Emmette S. Redford, "Business as Government," in Roscoe C. Martin, ed.,
Public Administration and Democracy: Essays in Honor of Paul H. Appleby
(Syracuse, N.Y.: Syracuse University Press, 1965), Chapter IV.

tive principle, that the intervention of the state should not be limited. There is still the danger that the administrative state will be loaded with more than it can do effectively, or more than it could do effectively without some arrangements for sharing functions with the private sector. It does suggest that preference for public-private federalism should be based on the incapacity of the public sector to handle all things rather than on undemocratic features that may exist within it.

The third concept is that public policy should aim toward solutions that can be carried into effect without discretionary administration. Policy should be self-executing, or executed through automatic administration. This is an element in the thought of neoliberal economic thinkers of our day.[5] They maintain that the state should adopt policies which either require little or no administration or which can be applied through administration programmed to operate according to stable rules. The rationale is that man is freer if he knows what rules he must adjust to, and that the economy will be more efficient if enterprisers can rely upon continuity and lack of discrimination in administration of public policy.

This viewpoint may be illustrated by reference to social policy for the aged. We have two systems. One—social security—provides virtually automatic administration and endows the individual with the security of a legal right. The other—aid to dependent aged—requires repeated checks by social workers into the intimate details of a person's life and leaves the individual dependent upon administrative judgment. It is not surprising that Milton Friedman, a leading neoliberal, should favor the negative income tax, for it would reduce the need for welfare administration based on an estimate of individual need.

5. For example of neoliberal literature in which this thought appears see Friedrich A. Hayek, *The Constitution of Liberty* (London: William Hodge and Co., 1960), pp. 224ff., and Carl J. Friedrich's essay on the first two volumes of Alexander Rüstow's major work *Ortsbestimmung der Gegenwart* (Erlenback-Zürick: E. Rentsch, 1952), in *The American Political Science Review*, XLIX (June 1955), pp. 509–25.

A further illustration of neoliberal administrative thought can be given by reference to housing policy. Neoliberals, it may be safely assumed, would prefer a system that gave higher wages to the poor than a system that gave rent subsidies, either through public housing or through rent supplements paid to private developers. The former policy can be largely self-executing, the latter requires administrative appraisals of individual need. Moreover, maintenance of income —in contrast to welfare aid for specific purposes—increases the capacity of the individual to cast effective ballots in the market place. It substitutes an increase in the democracy of the market place for public administration.

The neoliberal ideal is related to one expressed by a social-reform liberal years ago. Stuart Chase said during the Depression that broad, general ("bridge-head") public policies for the economy were preferable to those contemplated in plans for controlling production, prices, and wages.[6] This has been the view of those who sought monetary and fiscal solutions to problems of economic growth and stability and avoidance of detailed controls over production, wages, and prices. One can see that the former kind of policy involves less administration and less intimacy or meticulousness in the control over the economic enterpriser.

These ideas of economic conservatives (neoliberals) and economic liberals (social reformers) have a strong appeal. Administration programmed so as to limit the administrator to the application of rule can frustrate micropolitics, reduce invasions of privacy, ease the adjustment of the individual to public policy, reduce the problem of democratic control to one of overhead prescription of official duty, and simplify the problem of administrative effectiveness. And policy that minimizes administration—that, for example, guarantees minimum income rather than gives specific welfare payments, or that looks for generally operating economic measures

6. Stuart Chase, *A New Deal* (New York: The Macmillan Company, 1932). pp. 190–91.

(antitrust, collective bargaining, fiscal and monetary controls, guidelines on price and wage increases) instead of promotion and regulation of specific industries—may preserve the mixed economy, maintain freedom of choice for individuals on detailed matters, and reduce the magnitude of the problem of imbalanced representation of interests when policy is made selectively for areas where there is conflict between concentrated, high-quantity and diffuse, low-quantity interests. The student of administration, and of democracy, will find attractive elements in policy that either produces programmed administration, or achieves social goals with a minimum amount of administration and maximum retention of individual choice and adjustment.

Nevertheless, a high quantity of discretionary administration reaching into the details of life is unavoidable in most areas of policy. If one looks at such diverse functional areas as foreign affairs, education, minimum-wage guarantees, or protection of the quality of foods and drugs, he will see vast discretion in the administering authorities. Many authors have argued for increasing development of rules or standards in regulatory administration,[7] but all authorities recognize limitations on how far this can be carried. Policies often must be adjusted to special circumstances and new conditions and must therefore be flexible, as, for example, in the decisions of the Federal Reserve Board in response to variable circumstances. Reconciliation of interests that are in conflict must be delegated to administrative agencies. One factor that produces these necessities is the inability of those who make policy to find consensus on a general policy. Administration is often a result of the transfer of disagreements in policy from the macropolitical arena to administrative agencies.

This discussion supports three propositions about public affairs: First, we cannot escape the administrative state be-

7. For a particularly strong argument for extension of standards, see Henry J. Friendly, *The Federal Administrative Agencies: The Need for Better Definition of Standards* (Cambridge, Mass.: Harvard University Press, 1962).

cause it satisfies human needs, can deal comprehensively with interrelationships, and can claim to be more democratic than private administration. Second, public policy and public administration as its agent will have a dominant position in the concurrent public and private activities that form our public-private federalism. Third, the burden upon and the problems of the administrative state can sometimes be limited by policy choices that favor programmed administration or require a minimum of administration, but discretionary administration is an inescapable and necessary instrument for representation and adjustment of interests in the modern state.

WHAT IS THE NATURE OF THE ADMINISTRATIVE FUNCTION?

These comments, along with themes developed in the preceding chapters, lead us to the question: what kind of function or functions can we expect of the administrative state? All of the sophisticated discussion of administration in our day proceeds from two patterns of explanation about the nature of administration. In one, administration is thought of as *adjustive activity,* in the other as *directed activity.* My theses here are, first, that it is both and, second, that in this double quality one will find the ultimate issues of democratic administration.

In the concept of administration as adjustive activity, administration is an extension of the political process of adjustment among interests. The concept is reflected in many ways in our literature. The acceptance of the intermingling of politics and administration, common among students of public administration since Paul Appleby wrote *Policy and Administration* (1949),[8] leads to recognition that the adjustive process is continued in administration. The case studies resulting from the work of the Inter-University Case Committee have shown administrators "adjusting effectively to a highly

8. *Policy and Administration* (University, Ala.: University of Alabama Press, 1949).

complex environment composed of many forces" and making choices among values "that affect the well-being of society." [9] Discussions of congressional relations with administration have emphasized the coparticipation of committees and administrators in the continuous adjustment of interests. Analyses of private administration have supplemented our understanding of the adjustive function of executives. A former board chairman of the Standard Oil Company of New Jersey has described the primary goal in distributing income as maintaining "an equitable and working balance among the claims of various directly interested groups—stockholders, employees, customers, and the public at large." [10] James March has described the modern business executive as a broker of many interests. [11] And Chester I. Barnard, who wrote that the function of the executive was to unite men toward the attainment of a common purpose, [12] later described the executive as being controlled by multiple values. The actions of the executive, therefore, would necessarily be the result of the mediation of the values he was called upon to serve, rather than service to a single purpose or goal. [13]

Three pieces of literature may be cited as illustrating three aspects of the adjustive activity of administration. Pendleton Herring in *Public Administration and the Public Interest* (1936) wrote, "the purpose of the democratic state is the free reconciliation of group interests." This reconciliation would require a "great administrative machine" to synthesize the group interests into a unified conception of the public interest. A "harmonious relationship" between the bureaucracy

9. The quotations are from Harold Stein, ed., *Public Administration and Policy Development: A Case Book* (New York: Harcourt, Brace and Co., 1952), pp. xv and xvi.

10. Quoted in Edward S. Mason, ed., *The Corporation in Modern Society* (Cambridge, Mass.: Harvard University Press, 1959), p. 60.

11. James G. March, "The Business Firm as a Political Coalition," *The Journal of Politics*, Vol. XXIV (November 1962), pp. 662–78, particularly p. 672.

12. Chester I. Barnard, *The Functions of the Executive* (Cambridge, Mass.: Harvard University Press, 1938).

13. Chester I. Barnard, "Elementary Conditions of Business Morals," *California Management Review*, Vol. I (Fall 1938), pp. 1–13.

and the groups would be necessary for effective administration: "The solution of the liberal democratic state must lie in establishing a working relationship between the bureaucrats and the special interests—a relationship that will enable the former to carry out the purpose of the state and the latter to realize their own ends." [14] Herring's exposition has been followed by innumerable studies on the administrative function of *reconciling the interests outside administration*. These studies reflect in one way or another the group basis of politics and administration.

William Gore has emphasized the process of *internal adjustment within an organization*. He declares that today's organization "has more kinship with the model of the free market than with the model of a machine." [15] The organization as free market must respond both to environmental demands (external) and to purposes of men within the organization (internal). Because of this response an "organization pursues a great number of purposes concurrently," [16] including "formally stated, legitimized goals," professional goals and private ends of individuals within the organization, and the expectations of power centers outside the organization.[17] Organizations will "feel the equivalent of personality conflicts" because internal goals may "conflict with reality" or external circumstances "require internal adjustments that are difficult, sometimes impossible, to make." [18] As a result, tensions are created within the organization. These are emotional and the validation of a decision within the organization will depend upon factors "internal to the personality of the individual instead of external to it." [19] There must be a

14. *Public Administration and the Public Interest* (New York: McGraw-Hill Book Company, Inc., 1936). For the quoted words and other highly relevant passages, see pages 9, 16, 24, 25, and 259.
15. William J. Gore, *Administrative Decision-Making: A Heuristic Model* (New York: John Wiley & Sons, Inc., 1964), p. 119.
16. Ibid. p. 47.
17. Ibid. p. 37.
18. Ibid. p. 78.
19. Ibid. p. 12.

groping toward agreement, a search for what is acceptable within the organization. Moreover, "an organization is a multifunctional social mechanism [that maintains] some consistency between the values and goals of the productive groups housed within it,"—an "integrative mechanism" through which the "group objectives are fused into a meaningful whole." [20]

Charles Lindblom emphasizes the adjustive process *among organizations*. He extends the concept of the market place to the relationships among actors in strategic positions in the political-administrative system. Lindblom develops the thesis that mutual adjustment among partisans can be a means of co-ordination: "people can coordinate with each other without anyone's coordinating them. without a dominant common purpose, and without rules that fully prescribe their relations to each other." [21] He notes that as citizens we often co-ordinate our activities by mutual adjustment, as when an American coffee consumer and a Brazilian supplier are co-ordinated. He then proposes that we think of two alternatives for political action: central, synoptic, "directive" (my word) decisions and "mutual adjustment among political leaders" —"for example, in policy making by administrative agencies or in Congressional policy making, where one can imagine some central coordination by party leadership on the one hand, and mutual adjustment among legislators on the other." [22]

Lindblom describes specifically how partisan mutual ad-

20. Ibid. p. 155.
21. Charles E. Lindblom, *The Intelligence of Democracy: Decision Making Through Mutual Adjustment* (New York: The Free Press, 1965), p. 3.
22. Ibid. p. 11. Lindblom sees this as similar to his earlier concept of incremental decision, for in mutual adjustment each new decision is co-ordinated with past decisions. And this, in turn, is "at least an elementary form of rationality." *"For partisan mutual adjustment, therefore, to study coordination is to study rationality."* Finally, this is the democratic way: his book is entitled, *The Intelligence of Democracy.* For Lindblom's theory of incremental decision, see his "Policy Analysis," *American Economic Review,* Vol. XLVIII (June 1958), pp. 298–312, and his book (with David Braybrooke), *A Strategy of Decision* (Glencoe: Free Press, 1963).

justment is characteristic of the governmental process in this country:

> *Actual and potential legislators and executives, agencies, interest-group leaders, and party leaders constantly engage in partisan mutual adjustment with each other, both bilaterally and multilaterally, in all possible combinations.*
>
> *There is no highest prescriptive authority in government; no agency, legislator, executive, or continuing collectivity of legislators can prescribe to all others yet concede no authority to any other, even if indirect prescription is allowed for (the authority controls by prescribing that X prescribe to Z).*
>
> *No allocation of authority or function can be found that eliminates interdependence among participants in partisan mutual adjustment. . . .*[23]

Citizens, says Lindblom, are not direct participants in this process. It "occurs among decision makers, defined as a subset of all individuals." But adjustment among these decision makers, acting as partisans, is "ubiquitous." [24] While common values may "lay down some general lines of policy," partisan mutual adjustment among decision makers will often be the means by which they are given "practical application to concrete decisions." [25]

The three works chosen demonstrate, then, that modern commentators explain the adjustive process, with varying emphases, as encompassing groups outside organizations and interacting with them, men interacting within organizations, and organizations interacting with each other.

Perhaps few writers would describe administration solely in terms of adjustive activity.[26] Herring thought that adjust-

23. Ibid. pp. 98, 99, 100.
24. Ibid. p. 99.
25. Ibid. p. 132.
26. Perhaps Avery Leiserson came closest to this in his *Administrative Regulation: A Study in Representation of Interests* (Chicago: University of Chicago Press, 1942).

ment would require "a great administrative machine" and that government might find a standard for decision that would give it some independent weight among contending interests.[27] Appleby thought that the administrative process was not merely one of umpiring interests.[28] Gore said that "our administrative doctrine will now have a permanent duality"—recognizing both sanctioned patterns of structured behavior to achieve goals, and "indigenous patterns of accommodative behaviors."[29] Lindblom, arguing against full acceptance of pluralistic thought, concluded: "Partisan mutual adjustment, as seen here, is useful in some situations and not in others; a general endorsement of it seems as misplaced as a general condemnation."[30]

What is the other element in administration? *It is overhead direction of activity setting the preconditions of administration on the basis of some measure of consensus on what will be expected of it.* The direction and the expectations are included in four types of prescription: *purpose* is stated or implied, *organizations* are established, *rules* are prescribed, and by these means *roles* are created for actors within administration. The preconditions are amended in further overhead statement of purpose, structure, rules, and official roles. They are elaborated further for subordinate officials in the administrative hierarchy. All are embodied in practice in the roles of actors, and hence the summarization could be symbolized as POR→R (purpose, organization, rules, all producing roles).

These prescriptions bring administration into existence and set for it—with varying degrees of definiteness and compulsion—goals and patterns of activity. They give a substantial measure of guidance to it, and they establish tests of its

---

27. *Public Administration and the Public Interest*, pp. 6–9 particularly.
28. Paul H. Appleby, *Morality and Administration in Democratic Government* (Baton Rouge, La.: Louisiana University Press, 1952), p. 95.
29. *Administrative Decision-Making*, pp. 17 and 30.
30. *The Intelligence of Democracy*, p. 13.

legitimacy. While they do not entirely determine its activities, they are inescapable influences upon it. They place and direct man within administration, and they limit and confine the external impacts upon it.

Sometimes the result of directed administration is to establish a system that is strictly administrative, as, for example, in the social security program. At other times much is left open, but always there are some guides or cues for actors in standards of purpose and in rules. These provide something positive and substantive that prevents administrative activity from being merely or completely adjustive.

Administration, then, has two aspects. On the one hand, it is an extension of the process of social adjustment. Adjustments and choices among interests, initiated in the macropolitical system, are carried over into subsystems where interests are adjusted and choices made through the interaction of persons in strategic positions. Even within the separate organizations constituting the political-administrative subsystems, as in administrative agencies and Congressional committees, there is a brokerage of interests of persons operating within the organizations. Administration is, in this aspect of its performance, political.

But there is also something unique about administration. It is at every successive level subject to some direction from a higher authority. There is a difference between the wide-open adjustment of interests in the macropolitical arena, and the activity that follows the decision in that arena to set up a program for continuous implementation by administrative action. This difference is that at the heart of the subsystems growing out of the establishment of programs there are administrative agencies with *directions* to work at specific tasks, and that within these agencies standards fixing official roles direct and confine the activity of men at successive levels. Administration begins when the initial direction is given and it never escapes from its subordinate role.

What this means is that we have in administration an instrument for two types of service for society. By strict programming we can have automatic, continuing, nonpolitical activity in pursuit of goals on which there is consensus, except as this activity is returned to the macropolitical level for review, restraint, and support. Or by establishment of machinery with looser direction, we can have activity for continuous adjustment and choice among interests. Administration in its many activities ranges on a continuum between these types of activity. But for every level within administration there is some direction, and direction increases and discretion diminishes as activities are subdivided at successive levels. It is this quality of direction that gives administration its distinctive position in the political system.

These comments provide a clue for understanding the function of hierarchy. The latter will not eliminate adjustive activity both laterally and within organizations, though it may come close to this in some programmed activities. It cannot—by definition of official roles—eliminate the impact of personal stakes, societal standards, professional standards, and external pressures, though again it may reduce these to a minimum. It may move through multiple, even conflicting, channels, particularly at top levels. But it is a means of directing administration—of providing purpose, systematizing organization, and defining rules and official roles, and of enforcing these.

Hierarchy may be strong or weak in its sequential links, and the elements of strength and weakness fix the means of democratization of administration. To the extent that hierarchy is strong, and enforces a consensus (registered in policy, organization, and rules producing roles), then democratic controls can be exerted vertically through macropolitical lines. But to the extent that hierarchy is weak, conveys no firm consensus, and thus allows discretion in subsystems of interacting strategic centers, then democratic control can be maintained only through influences on the strategic subsystem centers.

WHAT CAN MAKE IT LEGITIMATE?

It may be argued that administration is legitimate in the same way weather is legitimate. One is as natural in society as the other is in nature. A more accurate statement, therefore, of the moral inquiry is: how can administration be *most fully legitimized?* To this question some may respond that it can be made legitimate by making the assumptions of overhead democracy effective in practice. But from the beginning of this book it has been assumed that administration is subject to many types of influence in addition to those exercised through the macropolitical structure.

Another answer is that it is *most fully legitimized if by all the processes of social control it conforms as fully as man can make it conform with the tenets of democratic morality.* This is a normative standard; it proceeds from the assumption that what man creates should be judged by what it does in response to his interests as reflected in his demands. Important additional assumptions are that the interests of all men are important and that man's interests are best protected and promoted when he, directly or through those representing him, participates in what has an effect on him.

Can we legitimize the administrative state through democratic control? Let us be clear, first, about the limitations on democratic control inherent in the administrative state. *Policy is made for and applied to us by minorities composed of men occupying strategic positions in specialized organizations, operating only in part under directives from organizations directly representative of the people.* Sometimes, moreover, there is secrecy, quick decision, and irrevocable decision. The processes of decision are so infinitely complex that they are elusive even to the best informed observer or researcher. The men who can participate in the decisions because they occupy strategic positions reflect in their behavior official roles and societal consensus but also personal stakes and special allegiances. Their decisions and actions bind us as subjects of administration and workers within administration. These things, as described in general in Chapter II and specifically as they operate in the American governmental system in Chapters III to VII, are inescapable.

We look nevertheless for means of realizing the democratic morality (which assumes the supremacy of the will of the governed) in the administrate state (which makes men subject to the decisions of others). We look, however, without utopian hope for full realization of the ideal in its pure form. Freedom through participation in all that affects an individual is not possible. The thoughtful person will be conscious of the fact that subjection to institutional power is not matched by his ability to control it through his action individually or co-operatively with those who share his interests. In social affairs, as with respect to nature, we start with the assumption that man does not have complete control over the conditions of his existence. We look, therefore, for a pattern of workable democracy. *Workable democracy may be defined as the most democracy that is achievable under the conditions that have produced the administrative state.* Workable democracy will be a set of processes through which there is maximum achievement of the democratic morality under limiting conditions. The processes establish a limited correspondence between the facts of the administrative state and the tenets of democratic morality.

The concept of workable democracy assumes a condition in which the interests of each and all are reflected in the totality of institutional operations. *Workable democracy is the inclusive representation of interests in the interaction process among strategic organizational centers—a representation resulting from the responsiveness of the interaction process in the totality of its parts and the totality of its decisions to the demands of men in an open society in which there is universal capacity for participation in meaningful ways.* This definition states the minimal requirements for processes that will satisfice as a concept of democracy. The interaction processes must provide inclusive representation, this must be the result of responsiveness to outer constituencies, these constituencies and the leaders in the strategic positions must operate in an open society, and the capacity (not merely the legal opportunity) to get into the game in some meaningful way must exist for the totality of the community.

The words "totality of its parts" and "totality of its decisions" in the definition of workable democracy merit special comment. The democracy of a political system cannot be denied on the basis of the elitism of some of its parts or on the basis of single decisions.[31] A political system is, as then Senator John F. Kennedy said, and as we have noted, a solar system. In such a system, elitist elements may in some instances compromise or negate democracy, and in other instances they may exist in a context of relationships that submerge, absorb, or checkmate their influence. A single decision may overextend the representation of some interests brought into convergence for that decision, and yet other decisions allocate advantages to other groups aggregated for influence on those decisions. The lack of balanced consideration of interests in the making of some decisions may be partially compensated by different balances in other decisions. The social system may be able to stand some degree of imperfection in the political system if the society is affluent and the system of control is loose enough to allow adjustments to it. And the accompanying deficiencies in the attainment of the democratic ideal may be acceptable in a concept of workable democracy if they are not too large or too prevalent in the political system.

Workable democracy must be achieved in part through the interactions within the leadership (or oligarchical) structure.

31. I am indebted to Paul H. Appleby for his insistence that we must judge the political system in "the totality of its parts." See Appleby, *Politics and Administration,* and *Morality and Administration in Democratic Government.*

The process of interaction can broaden the representation of interests. Pluralism within the leadership structure—the representation within it of different "estates"—can extend the inclusiveness of representation of interests. Moreover, the leadership may be forced by the complexity of problems to "trace things out as far as possible" before making a decision.[32] This too results in more interests being engulfed in the maelstrom of decision making. If rationality is defined as the consideration of all affected interests, then its pursuit by tracing things out is movement toward the democratic ideal.

But workable democracy requires also a kind of relationship between leaders occupying strategic positions and nonleaders affected by decisions made through interaction among strategic positions. It is a relationship that forces leaders to be responsive to nonleaders—that maximizes the subordination of personal leadership stakes and professional competence to directed purposes, rules, and roles, and to the total complex of interests seeking realization through direction of or representation in the process of adjustment of interests. This is only a way of saying in more precise terms that the interests of nonleaders must be represented in the action of leaders.

Workable democracy—indeed any concept of democracy—assumes positive response of leaders to nonleaders. It assumes that leaders will look for ways of implementing the interests of men in society. This does not mean that leaders will unhesitatingly assume burdens for the administrative state that it cannot effectively carry, but it does mean that they will be ready to implement the demands of men by whatever means they can devise. Workable democracy is antithetic to laissez-faire. It is not antithetic to the administrative state as a device for serving human interests.

In sum, workable democracy is achieved in public affairs

32. Arthur W. Macmahon, "Specialization and the Public Interest," in O. B. Conoway, Jr., ed., *Democracy in Federal Administration* (Washington, D.C.: Graduate School, U.S. Department of Agriculture, 1956), p. 49.

through the interaction of leaders of different types in strategic positions of influence, who are forced by the interaction process, the complexity of interests involved in a decision-making situation, and the access of nonleaders to their positions to give attention to all the interests in the society. Decisions are made in part at the macropolitical level, and the winning interests obtain continued representation through definition of purpose, organization, rules, and roles. They are made in part in the adjustive process that is continued in political-administrative subsystems, where choice, consensus, or compromise is achieved among conflicting and concurring interests represented through multiple channels.

Achievement of workable democracy is dependent upon the existence of a variety of features in the political system. First, there must be a macropolitical structure that is representative of men's common and diverse interests and that can reconcile these interests and convert them into directives to those who hold positions in the administrative structure. The directives define purpose, organization, and rules, and create official roles. They define—precisely or imprecisely, completely or partially—responsible activity within the administrative state.

Second, there must be a macroadministrative structure—i.e., top-level, continuous organizations with specialized functions—to enforce responsibility and to assist macropolitical leaders in extending, revising, or retracting directives to the subordinate administrative structure.

Third, since all activity will not be fully directed and adjustive capacity will be continued within the subordinate administrative institutions and allied structures, both public and private, affected interests must have effective access to these structures and rights of appeal from them. Some conflict between official roles, often created to represent diffused interests, and adjustive behavior, influenced constantly by concentrated, high-quantity interests, and between official roles and personal or professional stakes, can normally be expected at this subsystem level of activity. We have noted that one of the quandaries of democratic theory is the extent to which the diffused interests of many should have superiority over the high-quantity interests of a smaller number.

Fourth, since the dignity and right of each and every person is inherent in democratic morality, there must be special devices to protect man both as subject of administration and as worker within administration. There will be some conflict between program objectives embodied in macropolitical directives and the personal interests of men subject to administration or working within it; but here also democratic morality does not assume the complete supremacy of one kind of human interests over other kinds.

Fifth, since the structure of the administrative state, dispersing power among many centers, is complex, and since the interests of persons served by, subject to, and within administration are numerous, men must be free to set up organizations and create new leadership posts through which interests can be aggregated and meaningful access to strategic centers obtained. Private or quasi private organization through which group interests can be asserted is required for effective presentation of claims, and hence the open society which allows such organization is a prerequisite and continuing condition for workable democracy.

Finally, all must be able to participate meaningfully in politics. This means, first, no exclusions from the adult franchise other than the mentally defective or morally depraved. It means, second, that no group shall be deprived of the democratic freedoms of speech, organization, peaceable assembly, and peaceful demonstration. It means also something more positive, namely that all must be provided that amount of education, economic benefit, and status that will produce consciousness of capacity for individual fulfillment. Only men who are equipped with this consciousness of capacity will be able to make demands for their personal achievement. A society can be democratic only if the men within it are so conscious of their nobility and their interests that they are led, along with other men, to make claims for their own personal achievement. Acceptance of political inactivity resulting from lack of opportunity is avoidance of democracy; creation of universal ability for political activity extends the possibility of individual realization for all men.

Workable democracy, in short, depends upon pressure on and oversight over leaders from various parts of the society in ways sufficient to ensure their responsiveness. It presupposes a system that forces leaders to supersensitivity to the interests of all people—which forces them as they make policy to look for forming or formable consensuses and to give attention to the variety of conflicting and complementary interests within the society.

Workable democracy will be possible only if certain conditions exist within the society. It must be a humane society —one where there is general recognition of the dignity and integrity of each person. It must be an open society—one where any issue can be made the subject of public discussion and verdict, where even the crisis decision can be subsequently discussed and the responsible leaders subjected to democratic sanctions if their decision is unacceptable. It must be a society in which the ability and the will to participate are so widely distributed that leaders are kept sensitive to the interests of all. It must be a society in which men pursue decision making by search for consensus, by majority vote, and by brokerage of varied interests. It must be a society stable enough to supply well-understood institutional mechanisms and procedures for holding the balances among leaders and subjecting leaders to nonleaders, but it must also be flexible enough to allow new interests, or old interests newly recognized, to be asserted through new structures and new leaders.

For one who takes seriously the tenets of democratic morality, there are elements of both satisfaction and concern in the existence of the administrative state. It offers an opportunity to make effective use of the political system. We can make demands upon political leaders which lead them to direct the establishment of programs, organizations, rules, and roles through which our interests will be served. We can also gain structures through which our concurring and conflicting interests are continuously adjusted. Throughout our history there has been a tendency toward broadening the rights of participation by which effective demands can be made on political leaders, and we now can have hope that the political system will become truly responsive to the underprivileged of the past—the poor and the Negro. We can have hope, also, that those who serve in the administrative structure will generally act humanely both toward those subject to it and those working within it.

At the same time, there are many problems worthy of our concern. Categories of problems that appear to be most significant at this stage in our development can be listed:

1. The need for effective political participation by the ghetto residents and the rural poor;
2. The distortions in representation of the interests of the nation in the macropolitical structure;
3. The possibilities of imbalance of representation of interests in political-administrative subsystems;
4. The potentialities for fuller programming of micropolitical decisions on grants, contracts, or other benefits to communities and companies;
5. The possibilities for responses in public policy which call for minimum amounts of discretionary administration;
6. The threat of overextension of claims for secrecy in administration;
7. Threats to individual privacy;
8. Implementation of individual rights of subjects of and of workers within administration.

Different observers will assess differently the degree of correlation that exists or may exist between democratic morality and the operation of the administrative state in the United States. It is gratifying that most of the problems listed above are being earnestly discussed. It is gratifying, too, that our system as it emerges from this analysis contains in its broadest outlines a framework for workable democracy. It is gratifying, finally, that there are tendencies in the nation that, while alarming in some respects, nevertheless offer considerable hope for broader participation in a more humane, more open society.

Index

Absolutism, 176, 178

Acheson, Dean, cited, 74n

Administered society: central elements, 3; private structure, 184; public and private sectors, 182

Administration: access of the individual to, 141; achievement of democratic morality, 153; aspects of, 189, 194; congressional relations with, 78, 189; elements of protection for subjects of, 136–47, 193; high quantity of discretion, 187, instrument for two types of service for society, 194–95; of justice, 136–37; legitimacy of, 196–204; man as subject, 132–53; oversight of, 147; result of directed, 194; spirit, 134–35; systems, 94

Administrative agencies, 141, 149, 194

Administrative Conference of the United States, 148

Administrative function, nature of, 188–95

Administrative hierarchy, representation of farmers in administration at the bottom, 152

Administrative institutions, 30–31

Administrative law: opportunity to be heard, 136, 139–42; right to access, 139–42

Administrative organizations, 4

Administrative Procedure Act of 1946, 137, 140–41; framers, 142–43, 145

Administrative state: activities, 132; basic feature, 39–41; behavior, juxtaposed with American ideal of democracy, 4; concept of, 183; decision makers in, 53–65; interaction process in, 56; meaning, 30–31; official rules of organizations and persons in, 144; in perspective, 179–204; political-administrative system in Washington, 70–82: hazard of, 95–96; legitimacy of, 196–97; public policy and, 184–85; reason for having, 179–88; reflections on, 38–69; rules relating to employment in service of, 176–77

Administrative structures, recurring aspects of public functions to, 3

Administrative system, interaction in the national, 70–82

Administrators, field contacts of, 138

Adorno, T. W., cited, 15

Aged, social policy for, 185

Agger, Robert E., cited, 8n

Agricultural stabilization, functional complexes of interrelated interests in, 41

Agriculture, Department of, 125, 146

American Civil Liberties Union, 141

Antipoverty program, 152, 153

Appleby, Paul, cited, 184n, 188, 198n

Argyris, Chris, cited, 172, 173n

Aristotle, definition of citizen, 9

Associations, 181

Authoritarianism, 162–63, 178

Aviation, see Civil aviation

Ballot, the, 67–68; of the market place, 181, 182, 186

Barnard, Chester I., cited, 51n, 173n, 189